Justine Allain Chapman is an Anglican
vicar in south London, as a lecturer in p
while vice-principal of a theological i
England, and as Archdeacon of Boston
The role of adversity in healing and growt
speaks, leads retreats, and trains clergy and lay people. Justine lives with her husband Thomas near Lincoln with their four children.

THE RESILIENT DISCIPLE

A Lenten journey from adversity to maturity

Justine Allain Chapman

spck

First published in Great Britain in 2018

Society for Promoting Christian Knowledge
36 Causton Street
London SW1P 4ST
www.spck.org.uk

British Library Cataloguing-in-Publication Data
A catalogue record for this book is available from the British Library

ISBN 978–0–281–07853–0
eBook ISBN 978–0–281–07854–7

Typeset in India by Geethik Technologies
First printed in Great Britain by Ashford Colour Press
Subsequently digitally reprinted in Great Britain

eBook by Geethik Technologies

Produced on paper from sustainable forests

In memory of my mother, Eileen Chapman,
who was brave, generous and full of tales

Contents

Introduction

Some time ago, keen to know what helped people come through adversity so well that they were stronger, more loving and wiser, I took myself off to study that whole area, under the title of resilience.

Resilience is the ability to bounce back or be strengthened in response to the adversities of life. It has become a popular theme because it focuses on developing the qualities we need to come through, rather than on the things that bring us down. The study I undertook, of course, came out of my own experience of life and its ups and downs as well as the lives of others whom I'd been alongside and sought to support in my ministry as a parish priest and theological educator. The work I did, and a book I wrote, led to me leading retreats and speaking at events. What struck me was that to incorporate some of the insights that resilience literature offers to us into our thinking and praying and living is best done gradually, over a period of time.

Six weeks is a good period of time, it is said, to break bad habits and establish some new ones in our patterns of thinking and our actions. So, the season of Lent seemed to lend itself to the contemplation of adversity and being strengthened by God through it. The 40 days of Lent mark the period of time in which Jesus retreats into the wilderness or desert, driven there by the Holy Spirit, to struggle with the temptations of the devil. The season of Lent, ending as it does with Holy Week, lends itself to finding our hope and life in following the pattern that Christ sets as he faces suffering and death, trusting in God to bring about life.

I have called this book *The Resilient Disciple* because for me (as for many Christians) it is the journey through the difficulties of life that has strengthened my faith and deepened my discipleship. This book seeks to take the reader through a process, or on a journey, enabling us to go deeper in reflecting on the adversities of life in order to be strengthened to meet adversity ahead and to live out compassion now.

In earlier research that I undertook into resilience I identified three themes that are key to being strengthened. They are *struggle*, *self* and *relationships*, and growing in them, through adversity, sets a path towards altruism or compassion. This is often expressed in people's lives by taking up pastoral responsibility or becoming involved in working for justice or social action.

My hope and prayer is that these reflections might help us to pray into current experiences of adversity in such a way as to help us embrace the struggle, connect with ourselves and focus on holding fast to healthy relationships. This task of reflection, in the presence of God, will help us to integrate our experiences. By doing this we can find a deeper healing, a letting go and an inner strength from which to follow Christ.

The shape of the book

As you begin this journey through Lent I invite you to read each reflection and take from it what is pertinent to you. I have chosen a prayer for the morning and the evening and a prayer of protection or peace for each week, for you to use in that week. The themes within them will resonate with the reflections. I have also chosen a verse from the twenty-third psalm, a psalm you may want to carry through this Lent. There are no Sunday reflections because Sundays are not part of the 40 days of Lent, but you could read the introduction to the week on Sundays if you wish to read daily.

The reflections for the first two weeks are entitled Follow and Flourish because they focus on discipleship. In the next three weeks, Falling, Faithful and Fruitful each take an experience from the life of that resilient disciple, Peter. Fulfil focuses on the pattern Christ sets for us in the events of Holy Week.

We begin with **Follow**, as Jesus does, in the hardship of the desert, trying to make a straight path through it, a way for God.

Continuing in the second full week of Lent with **Flourish**, the focus is on the themes of embracing the struggle, attending to and resourcing the self, and forging healthy relationships. These resilience themes are woven into the reflections.

The theme of **Falling** for week three explores our brokenness. Peter is the resilient disciple who falls when he denies he knows Jesus three times, at his point of real need.

Jesus had prayed that Peter's faith would not fail, and in week four, in **Faithful**, we reflect on the way in which crisis provides a crossroads where God's faithfulness can open us to light, healing and restoration. Peter is asked three times by Jesus whether he loves him and is called again to follow.

In week five, in **Fruitful**, we reflect on the expansion of compassion and wisdom shown in those who have come through adversity. For Peter, his experience of the vision of a tablecloth coming down three times from heaven prompts him to cross cultural and religious boundaries and to preach to Gentiles, revealing God's love for all the nations of the world.

Holy Week is the final week of Lent, and in **Fulfil** we see that it is in following the pattern of the life, death and resurrection of Jesus that we experience passing from difficulty and death to healing, light and life in Christ.

At the back of the book I have provided suggestions for reading the reflections as a group as well as suggestions for worship leaders and preachers.

FOLLOW: FROM ASH WEDNESDAY AND THROUGH THE FIRST WEEK OF LENT

> He leads me in right paths for his name's sake.
> (Psalm 23.3)
>
> Surely goodness and mercy shall follow me
> all the days of my life,
> and I shall dwell in the house of the LORD
> my whole life long. (Psalm 23.6)

As we begin Lent we follow Jesus into the wilderness of the desert and remain there with him for 40 days and 40 nights. The desert was a real place of hardship for Jesus and also the place of inner struggle where he was tempted not to follow God but to follow the ways of evil. For us, too, the desert is a real place we could go to, but it is also a metaphor for adversity. People commonly talk about 'desert experiences' when life has been empty and difficult, the way hard and the outcome uncertain.

In adversity, we follow advice in the unknown territory. This advice will be from professionals, such as doctors, and others who know us well, and gradually we internalize or incorporate into our lives what helps us. The change of the circumstances of our lives may well have set external parameters for our path, but we must also attend to our inner life. We will need to find a solid place among the shifting sands on which to stand and to find refuge, in God as our rock.

At first, we can only go one step at a time as we seek to cope with the challenge of difficulty. John the Baptist, already in the wilderness, will advise us to make a direct path through this landscape. In a deserted landscape, Jesus heard and remembered, as we do, different voices. We will need to choose who to listen to. 'I have set before you life and death, blessings and curses,' says the Lord. 'Choose life' (Deuteronomy 30.19). We will be accompanied by desert Christians of the fourth and fifth centuries, *abbas* and *ammas*, whose 'Sayings' have been collected to offer wisdom to disciples; their translation is by Sister Benedicta Ward in *The Sayings of the Desert Fathers: The Alphabetical Collection* (Mowbray, 1975).

As we set a path and begin, we will experience life and goodness surging up and calling us personally and specifically, as those first disciples did. Peter was renamed when he heard Jesus' call to follow, with a name he would grow into by responding to the call to a deep relationship with Jesus.

This is what Lent invites us to: a deeper, simpler kind of discipleship that involves some austerity or discipline and will strengthen us so we mature and grow in compassion and wisdom.

The psalmist, at the beginning of the twenty-third psalm, reminds us that by following the shepherd we will be led along the right path. The care given by the shepherd, the psalmist realizes by the end of the psalm, is expressed not only in following, but in experiencing goodness and mercy following us.

Prayers for the week

For the morning

Almighty and everlasting God,
we thank you that you have brought us safely
to the beginning of this day.
Keep us from falling into sin
or running into danger,
order us in all our doings
and guide us to do always
what is righteous in your sight;
through Jesus Christ our Lord.
(A morning collect from *Common Worship*)

For the evening

Be present, merciful Lord, and protect us through the silent hours of this night, so that we who are wearied by the changes and chances of this fleeting world may rest upon your eternal changelessness, through Jesus Christ our Lord. (From the Leonine Sacramentary)

Prayer of St Columba

Be a bright flame before me,
a guiding star above me.
Be a smooth path below me,
a kindly shepherd behind me,
today, tonight and for ever.

Serenity prayer

God grant me the serenity
to accept the things I cannot change;
courage to change the things I can;
and wisdom to know the difference.
(Reinhold Niebuhr, 1892–1971)

Words from Scripture

You search out my path and my lying down,
and are acquainted with all my ways.
(Psalm 139.3)

See if there is any wicked way in me,
and lead me in the way everlasting.
(Psalm 139.24)

A psalm to read

Psalm 139

Ash Wednesday: enter the desert

And the Spirit immediately drove him out into the wilderness. He was in the wilderness for forty days, tempted by Satan; and he was with the wild beasts; and the angels waited on him. (Mark 1.12–13)

Remember you are dust and to dust you shall return. Turn away from sin and be faithful to Christ.
(Traditional words for the ashing of penitents on Ash Wednesday)

A few years ago, I spent an eight-day retreat in the Egyptian desert. The desert is a vast and beautiful landscape. The colours of the sky and the sand, the piercing blue against the reds and yellows, are intense. It always was and it still is difficult to live there, for little grows. During the day it is hot, and walking on sand is hard work. At night, sleeping under the stars, it is very cold. Rocks and mountains provide shelter from the wind and shade from the sun. Alone in the desert you are forced to focus on how you will survive. Survival is a struggle and if you don't monitor your thirst and your water supply, the effects of the heat and cold will ensure you won't live very long.

We can experience the deserts of the world today in much the same way as human beings for many centuries, and we can learn the same lessons. St Anthony (*c.* 251–356), who spent many years as a hermit in the desert, spoke of the desert as a great teacher. The Holy Spirit, after Jesus' baptism, drove him into the wilderness or desert for 40 days and 40 nights. There, like many before him and since, he struggled with temptation and emerged strengthened.

Throughout history, people have sought God in the desert landscape, whether they have fled there because they needed to escape like Moses, Hagar and Elijah, or because like John the Baptist and Jesus they needed a space to discern God's way forward for their lives. In the fourth and fifth centuries many Christians, the most famous of these being St Anthony, went to the desert alone or to live in communities with others because they wanted to be challenged to grow in faith. They experienced desert life as a physical, spiritual and mental training in faith. They were inspired by St Paul's image of the disciple training like an athlete (1 Corinthians 9.24–27). There are many Sayings remembered and collected by people who went to visit these desert Christians for a word of advice. These Sayings are full of what we call 'the wisdom of the desert'.

You don't have to go to the desert to have a desert experience, though, do you? There are times in our lives when we realize that we are in a different territory because the terrain of our lives has become harder to navigate. There are problems or situations that it's time to face and deal with. Some of us are inclined to panic, and some go into denial, pretending nothing is wrong. In the desert, we won't survive if we pretend there is nothing we need to attend to. We cannot be like an ostrich sticking its head in the sand. Nor can we panic, rushing around and wasting energy.

We know that many of life's challenges are not solved overnight and that change and growth will take time. There is a process to undergo, a journey to make to get through the difficulty and out through the other side. The desert experience can come upon us suddenly in the form of illness, a damaged relationship or bereavement. We might seek to enter the desert as a place to examine a destructive pattern in our lives that needs to change, to pray over an important decision, or for some time and space to retreat and be open to God.

In Lent, the Church invites us to follow Christ into the desert for a season, for 40 days and nights. In solidarity with Jesus we will expect to struggle with temptations and demons, deepen in prayer and be ministered to by angels along the way. Though this is a personal journey we are not alone, for no one can survive the desert without the support of others. For me, it was the Bedouin who provided water and orientation as they have done for pilgrims over the centuries and as ravens did for Elijah. Jesus went with the crowds to his cousin John, who knew the power of the desert and so drew people out there to hear him preach the nearness of God. Emerging from the desert, Jesus went to choose those who would be his companions, his disciples. We will have companions too on this journey, some known, some yet to be discovered.

We will find the desert a place of struggle, fear and uncertainty, but also a place of beauty, solace and clarity. It is a distinct territory, austere and with clear boundaries. Time in the desert shapes us, first by reminding us that we are fragile, mortal, of dust and will return to dust. The habits we have to develop to stay alive here teach us how to survive and enable us to grow. On Ash Wednesday, the ash put on our foreheads is put in the shape of the cross, the mark of our salvation. The experience of the desert evokes the pattern of the life, death and resurrection of Christ. We are shaped by Christ.

In this season of 40 days we will be shaped by our contemplation of desert experiences, now and in the past, and will come through strengthened. We will be shaped by our deepening relationship with God. Whether you embrace the season or find yourself surprised to be here, choose how you will mark this territory and ask God for grace to be faithful to Christ.

- May I encourage you to mark out your own territory in space and time? You may have decided to give something up to mark Lent. You might find something where you sit, or in a place you pass by, which reminds you of the territory you are in and that you seek to grow – perhaps a picture of a desert, some dry twigs or stones.

Thursday: make a straight path

A voice cries out:
'In the wilderness prepare the way of the Lord,
make straight in the desert a highway for our God.
Every valley shall be lifted up,
and every mountain and hill be made low;
the uneven ground shall become level,
and the rough places a plain'. (Isaiah 40.3–4)

In those days John the Baptist appeared in the wilderness of Judea, proclaiming, 'Repent, for the kingdom of heaven has come near.'
(Matthew 3.1–2)

I love to see the bulbs in early spring, beginning with the white of snowdrops, when it is really still winter, then the yellow of daffodils and much later the varied colours of the tulips. The word 'Lent' comes from 'lengthening', and as the days get longer I can see what has been hidden by the darkness of winter. I know, when I look in the garden, that there is unwanted growth and the bulbs have pushed their way up through debris that I need to clear away. The old leaves I've left from autumn need to go and I must clear a way through tangled shoots and new weeds, if any flowers more delicate than spring bulbs are to emerge.

Lent provides the opportunity to clear a path in our lives for God. We might leave sorting out the garden for a few weeks, but in Lent we follow Jesus into the desert and there we need to find a path to God more quickly, for survival is an issue. The desert is a disorientating place and it is difficult to discover which way to go because all you can see is land and sky. Isaiah and John the Baptist recommend preparing a straight way through the desert, and a levelling of the path, so that you can travel most safely and quickly through difficult terrain. The desert terrain is not only vast and hard to cross, even on a camel, but also everything has to be carried, since you have to make your own camp at night – there are no hotels to check into.

In new and challenging territory, such as an unwelcome difficulty, or the discipline of Lent, we have to work out how to survive, how to live and flourish. That means clearing away what will distract us and impede new growth, and focusing on how to find a path through. We have to forge a way through any desert experience, often without much of a map. To make a straight path through, by the most direct route, you have to leave behind what you no longer need. There are times when clearing out is done for us by events – such as a death or diagnosis – that have created a hole in our lives. We have to take stock of what resources we have to meet the present situation. Self-awareness is the quality that enables us to recognize where we are, what has changed for us and what to do now. Some self-discipline will enable us to take the first steps to do it. John the Baptist invited his hearers to repent in order to avoid the inevitable consequences of judgement. The invitation was to change before it was too late and the consequences were already upon them. He told them that the kingdom of God was near and so they should prepare a way for the Lord.

If I don't pay attention and sort out my overgrown garden then it'll get worse. If I don't clear a space in my life to rest, think my own thoughts or be creative, my stress will become distress and quite possibly lead to illness of some sort. Now is the time to pay attention to our lives and journey through Lent aware of the need for change, which John calls repentance, a turning towards God.

Resilience is generally accepted as involving three Cs: Coping, being Constant, and Constructing. We need to be resilient in the face of challenging circumstances or adversities. In order to bounce back, recover or come through well, we will need to make changes in our lives. Adversity may be thrust upon us, seemingly from nowhere. Sometimes we are aware of poor choices in the past having an impact and at other times we take up a challenge in order to increase our strength in some way. Two desert virtues, attention and simplicity, help us here. We need to be attentive to the new circumstances, and to the impact on ourselves. To cope with the changes, we will need to set a path and priorities that have a simplicity about them. Forced by the need to survive and come through to be strengthened in difficulty, we are required to change.

Resilient people, those who have come through difficulty well, report a journey that has a moral direction. It starts in adversity and ends in altruism, for the fruits of the journey of suffering are experienced as compassion for others and healing for oneself. It is a costly journey, or we might say a narrow rather than a broad way, where the choice is between life and death, what is life-giving and what tends to destruction.

John the Baptist is austere in his demand that we make a way for the Lord, but also reminds us that God is near. He used Isaiah's words to talk about travelling through the desert. 'Comfort, O comfort my people' is what Isaiah is told to do by God (Isaiah 40.1). John heralded the coming of the Messiah and points us to Jesus. We need to forge a straight path and also remember that Christ described himself as the Way, the Truth and the Life (John 14.6).

Being baptized by John marked a person's commitment to God and to live a righteous life. It involved a physical cleansing for a new task. The marking of a new season or knowing what needs to be done to recover health can bring energy and purpose. Asking for help opens us to a path that is life-giving and one where we can expect to experience God's presence. Jesus queued up to be baptized by John and experienced the voice of God affirming him and the Holy Spirit dwelling in him.

- As you begin Lent you might like to pay attention to what fills your life and see whether you can clear a path that enables you to gain some simplicity. I have often found it valuable to take a large piece of paper and write my name in the centre. In pencil I write down all the things I can think of that fill my life. I include responsibilities, work, pleasures, people, domestic tasks. I then go over in red the things that drain me and in green the things which nourish me. What is neutral I go over in blue. Attentive to the balance, I seek ways of making changes to enable me to live with a simplicity that means I can choose life.

Friday: voices in the silence

> You are my Son, the Beloved; with you I am well pleased.
> (Luke 3.22)
>
> If you are the Son of God, command this stone to become a loaf of bread. (Luke 4.3)
>
> Be still, and know that I am God!
> (Psalm 46.10)

The desert landscape endures, and this, along with the vastness, is a potent reminder of the smallness and vulnerability of the human being. I was surprised at how noisy the desert is, so that even if I shouted, I could not make myself heard above the noise of the wind. When everything was still, the terrain was so big there was no one who would be near enough to hear me. I couldn't make an impact on the place; I was silenced.

Beauty can render us speechless, but shock, fear and trauma can silence us, sending us inwards, so we cannot speak. The desert, when there is no wind, is still and silent. Silence is part of what the desert teaches, but it is a process beginning with being silenced. When we are quiet it is common to experience a lot of inner noise, chatter and even self-accusation, and finally a deep silence within. It is rare that we experience silence in the course of our daily lives. In the quietness of walking or gardening we may mull life over in a way that can be creative, but there are other times, especially when we are vulnerable or tired, when quietness can be destructive. Two of the biggest factors that impede our mental health are rumination and self-blame. The desert experience gives us time, space and the need to face our demons, or destructive thoughts. We need our mental wits about us in order to survive there and so we learn to be alert to what is going on within us.

When we pause and free our minds from distraction, one of the things we do is to remember and go over things that we have said and things that have been said to us. We can feel our hearts become warm and lift when we recall a compliment. We can also be dashed down by an abrasive comment or casual criticism. Sometimes what we remember has happened recently and it disappears, but there are also things that persistently return, perhaps words that were said years ago and have stayed with us. We are all shaped by our experiences and relationships, and if we have had an imbalance of negative influences in some aspect of our lives, our thoughts can easily find destructive pathways. These thoughts are the demons of the desert experience and we have to face them to overcome them. The memories of those who have known and loved us also shape us, and though we might find them harder to remember when we are low, we can continue to draw strength from the words and actions of these people. When we find that positive comments can slide out of our minds easily but negative comments keep returning, we need to take note of this and redress the balance in a deliberate way. This will involve turning our mind away from what is destructive by feeding it with what is true about us, that we are loved by God, have hope and a future. Some people memorize a verse from the Bible or a short prayer to repeat at such times.

At the beginning of Lent we read that Jesus enters the wilderness having just been baptized and with the voice of God's love ringing in his ears. It didn't take long, however, before Jesus had to decide who to listen to and who to follow. He could hear the voice of his Father at his baptism and in the desert, and the voice of the devil who tried to tempt him away from being true to who he was. The pull towards God was expressed when Jesus sought out John the Baptist in the wilderness of the River Jordan and responded to John's invitation to mark his desire to live for God by being baptized. Jesus experienced God's nearness and the goodness of God towards him. He hadn't done anything special as yet, but he heard God's voice assuring him that he belonged – 'you are my Son and that gives me pleasure'. It is the voice of God for each of us in baptism where we are made children of God in Christ. The pull away from God came in the form of the temptation to doubt God's voice, be tempted not to trust God but to prove it: 'If you are the Son of God, command this stone to become a loaf of bread', said the devil.

In the desert Jesus faced his demons, the things that would draw him away from dwelling in the love of God and fulfilling the call God was making on his life. Having looked them in the face he was strengthened to know himself and them, and to choose his path.

The Holy Spirit had led or driven Jesus into the desert, for there was prayer and decision-making for Jesus to do regarding his future. He needed to consider who he was, how he should use his talents and which people he should choose to be with him. This he did, for when he emerged he began his ministry, chose 12 disciples, and started preaching and healing.

The inner noise and chaos gives way to persistent voices. Growing in resilience involves remaining Constant, the second C, and resisting the pull of an inner, undermining narrative. Are they demons or angels, leading us away from God or messengers of God? Peace comes when we choose what is life giving.

Many people of prayer practise silence in order to be still and open before God. Most commonly it is awareness of and attention to our breathing that brings an inner silence. A sigh reveals to us our weariness with some aspect of life, taking a deep breath our readiness for the next thing. Noticing our breathing and slowing it when we are anxious can bring self-awareness and calm. Mindfulness and the practice of meditation have become very popular and many Christians practise silence through meditation or contemplation. By becoming aware of your breathing for a period of time you connect with and accept yourself, and you notice your thoughts without engaging with them. When we are conscious of our breath and fully present to ourselves we can come to God with our needs and more clearly hear his voice.

- Are you aware of voices from the past that have shaped your life? Could you identify some that have inspired or encouraged you, some that shocked you with a truthfulness and care that helped you grow, any that still have the power to bring you down? Which memories will inspire you today?
- Sit for a few minutes today being attentive to your breathing. Might the practice of silence enable you to hear God's voice within you?

Saturday: solid as a rock

The Lord is my rock, my fortress, and my deliverer,
my God, my rock in whom I take refuge,
my shield, and the horn of my salvation, my stronghold.
(Psalm 18.2)

The name of the Lord is a strong tower;
the righteous run into it and are safe.
(Proverbs 18.10)

When I am able to be still – before the horizon, in a silent church or in front of a fire – I often find I sigh out my breath and breathe in the quiet beauty before me. I did this at times in the desert, but I also felt panic when waking alone, not knowing where to go or what to do to get out of the wind. The setting was still and beautiful, but it is a landscape that doesn't care for living things. The desert is immense, while I am small; dry, where I need moisture. It has been the death of so many travellers who lost their way and could find no relief.

Once calm enough, having slowed my breathing, I looked around the desert. The landscape then changed before my eyes from being indifferent to providing places of support, even comfort. After a while I realized that there were rocks that I could sit on and rest. I could stand firm on them or climb for a bit to avoid the tiring walking through sliding sand. The rocks were places I could shelter from the wind and find coolness in the sun. If I looked around me and looked carefully, I could see that although the landscape was indifferent and inanimate, it was able to provide comfort and shelter. As a child my little sister, usually while doing her maths homework, would slump across the kitchen table and cry, 'Nobody helps me!' In a long-division panic she wasn't calm enough to see that help was at hand. Nor had I been.

To find support from the landscape I had to pay attention to myself and know I needed to be calm enough to think. Then I could pay attention to what was in front of me. The psalmist uses the image of rock as an image for God. God is a rock, a hiding place, a refuge and a strong tower. God is present and yet there are times when we don't call on God or pray in such a way that we recognize our need of God and seek shelter.

Realizing we are vulnerable might well cause us to act. There are times when we need to look after ourselves by seeking protection. That might mean withdrawing or hiding away for a few minutes during a meeting, or for longer periods, regularly, to recoup. In Genesis, Hagar flees, pregnant, to the desert because it is a refuge from the bullying jealousy of her mistress Sarah. There she finds the space to work out what her options are. She meets with God, learns of the future for her unborn child, and is strengthened physically and spiritually. Her words show that she feels she has really been heard and so that is the name she gives her son:

> And the angel of the LORD said to [Hagar], 'Now you have conceived and shall bear a son; you shall call him Ishmael, for the LORD has given heed to your affliction . . .' So she named the LORD who spoke to her, 'You are El-roi'; for she said, 'Have I really seen God and remained alive after seeing him?'
>
> (Genesis 16.11, 13)

Hagar knows that she has seen God and she returns to the difficult household, ensuring safety for Ishmael and herself for the time being.

Just as God is a refuge, so are physical spaces, and the desert itself can be a refuge. The 'desert Christians' spoke of the need to flee to the desert. Some relationships draw us down a destructive road, undermine us and our well-being, and so fleeing might be necessary, or at least a lessening of contact. Though it is difficult without the supports even destructive relationships can bring, the hardship, like the desert, can provide refuge and the space to breathe.

Praying silently with our breathing calms and steadies us. Hurt by harsh words, or conflict, I have found that praying wordlessly with the image of God as a strong tower has helped me to be less defensive, because I sensed that I am defended. Imagining God as a tower that I can hide in has given me a breathing space. Present there, protected from the heat of the conflict or the storm and wind, I can experience being protected by the solidity of the tower. Sometimes I find I am curled up at the bottom of the tower in the heat of the day, so am soothed and cool because of the rock. After a time of praying with this picture, I have experienced being able to climb the steps within the tower and look out over the situation I have withdrawn from with new perspective, from a place of safety – the love and care of God.

It can be hard when you are in the midst of difficulty to discover a place of safety. Withdrawing to God, a stable and solid rock, might be the work of a moment, like sheltering from a shower under a bus shelter until it passes and you continue on your way. It might be a much longer process of staying with and working on your issues. In one of the Sayings of the desert Christians, Amma Syncletia speaks about the need to face ourselves and our lives:

> If you find yourself in a monastery do not go to another place, for that will harm you a great deal. Just as the bird who abandons the eggs she was sitting on prevents them from hatching, so the monk or nun grows cold and their faith dies, when they go from one place to another.

She promises that new life will emerge if we have the patience to stay with our stuff, just as a hen needs to sit on the eggs until new life emerges.

- You might like to pray wordlessly, imagining yourself approaching God who is a rock, a refuge or strong tower.
- If you haven't chosen a charity to support during Lent, you might like to give to one that provides refuge – perhaps a women's refuge or a charity supporting refugees.

Monday: called to depth

When [Jesus] had finished speaking, he said to Simon, 'Put out into the deep water and let down your nets for a catch.' Simon answered, 'Master, we have worked all night long but have caught nothing. Yet if you say so, I will let down the nets.' When they had done this, they caught so many fish that their nets were beginning to break.

(Luke 5.4–6)

Then Jesus said to Simon, 'Do not be afraid; from now on you will be catching people.' When they had brought their boats to shore, they left everything and followed him. (Luke 5.10–11)

Young wizards and witches from Muggle families received their invitation to study at Hogwarts School for Witchcraft and Wizardry out of the blue, literally, via an owl. This, of course, is in the magical world created by J. K. Rowling in her stories of the exploits of Harry Potter and his friends Ron Weasley and Hermione Grainger. Although the invitation to study at Hogwarts was completely unexpected for someone from a Muggle, or non-wizarding, family, realizing they were magical made sense of the odd things these children found they could do. For Harry Potter, an orphan, arriving in the magical world gave him a sense of belonging and an inner dignity that he had never before experienced. The books and films about Harry Potter have shaped an entire generation, opening up a glorious parallel world. It's a world where Harry's friendship with Ron and Hermione, his loyalty to Dumbledore, the sacrificial love of his mother, and his own courage give him what he needs to fulfil his call, which is to overcome the evil facing his world.

We often imagine the scene of Jesus walking on the shore calling 'Follow me' and the fishermen dropping everything. Even a slightly closer reading of the stories of the call makes us realize that there was a process of invitation and response with the disciples weighing Jesus up, listening to him speak, discovering that he could heal Peter's mother-in-law and then give them unsolicited advice about where they should fish. It was after a night of fishing when they had caught nothing that Jesus wanted to borrow their boat to stand in and preach from while they cleaned their nets. Catching nothing mirrored their sense of emptiness and oppression. It is often at such times that we are more open to seeing and responding to an invitation to take a new path. We are low and struggle to find a way through, a way to cope. We follow advice that might help us. Perhaps the disciples thought there was nothing to lose, so when Jesus led them to fish in a different place it wasn't too hard to give it a try.

The huge haul of fish, however, indicates that we follow Jesus not just out of our emptiness and need but also because of God's blessing on our lives. The experience of goodness and mercy following us opens us to the deeper life of meaning and of God. The successful catch of fish meant that the disciples didn't leave for a new life having failed in their old profession. They could move from catching fish to catching people, recognizing that Jesus, who had guided them to a huge catch of fish, could be trusted to guide them in forming a movement of people ready for the new thing that God would do. In calling them to catch people, Jesus affirmed their experience and saw their skills as transferable.

The actual call to follow, like a Hogwarts' owl, was out of the blue and each chose to respond by following Jesus. Jesus called Peter and the other fishermen, not to a parallel world but to a deeper life in God. The call made sense of their hunger for something more to life than what they were experiencing, but blessed and honoured who they were and what they brought with them.

Disciples follow the one who leads them, but just as they do not follow blindly, they do not follow alone but find others following too. When we count our followers on social media we can go into the hundreds and even the thousands. These people don't know one another, of course, any more than guests at a wedding who represent disparate parts of two people's lives.

When Jesus called these early disciples to follow him, it was an invitation to a real relationship, not only with him but also with each other. One of the things that come through so strongly in the world of Harry Potter is that Harry, Ron and Hermione overcome evil and fear because they are bound to each other in friendship. The story of the defeat of Lord Voldemort is also the story of their increasing trust in and respect for one another. It is their loyalty to their head teacher Dumbledore and openness to goodness itself that means they are provided with what they need just when they need it. Harry can fulfil his call only in relationship to everyone else. Ron is jealous of Harry's fame, but for Harry being a celebrity is empty. It is having family and friends that makes his life whole.

The plural of 'disciple' is 'church'. The call to follow Christ is one that brings us closer to other followers, those we have a natural affinity to – other people who go fishing perhaps – and those we don't. As we build trust and respect in our churches with real relationships, we can release gifts in ourselves and in others that we didn't know we had. The blessing came for Peter because he responded to Jesus' call to go deeper and in doing so had to call on others to help with all the fish.

When Peter cast the nets into deeper water and had to get help with the huge catch of fish he felt overwhelmed, unclean, and was unsure about Jesus, saying, 'Go away from me, Lord, for I am a sinful man.' When we go deeper, personally and in faith, much can come to the surface. There will be more to consider and handle and others to work with, as Peter found. Going deeply as a person and as a Christian always opens us up to God and to other people, and it can be frightening and uncomfortable. Simon Peter wants Jesus to go away and leave him alone. For a moment he'd rather live a small life, one where he feels safe, because now he feels overwhelmed and sinful – not up to a bigger vision, the more generous life that Jesus calls him to.

These early disciples of Jesus were chosen by him and made a choice to follow in such a way as to bring about a huge change of life. Following Jesus from a place of depth, with other disciples, will bring change and growth. In church, as individuals, we follow Jesus from different starting places, as cradle Christians and converts, knowing that like the 12 disciples we are called together. Like an apprentice, we learn wisdom and compassion from being around those who are wise and loving.

- Do you have a friend, mentor or spiritual director whom you might arrange to see, and consider where you are being called from and what to?

Tuesday: named

> But now thus, says the LORD,
> he who created you, O Jacob,
> he who formed you, O Israel:
> Do not fear, for I have redeemed you;
> I have called you by name, you are mine.
> (Isaiah 43.1)

> [Andrew] brought Simon to Jesus, who looked at him and said, 'You are Simon son of John. You are to be called Cephas' (which is translated Peter). (John 1.42)

> And I tell you, you are Peter, and on this rock I will build my church, and the gates of Hades will not prevail against it. (Matthew 16.18)

Estate agents recommend that when a prospective buyer comes round to view your house, you should have some coffee percolating; apparently this creates an aroma and atmosphere conducive to a sale. Coffee shops have become increasingly popular and each chain wants to provide for your every need. This extends to giving you not only your preferred type of coffee but also an entire experience. In some cafés, a barista will ask for your name and write it on the cup. I like to give a false name and when I'm in the queue, usually at a train station, I wonder: *Who shall I be today?* It's a bit of fun to give another name, to challenge my own imagination and identity for a moment, as long as I remember who I said I was when the coffee is ready to collect.

What assumptions and expectations go with your name? Some people change their name or the form of it at different stages of life or at work, or socially. Our surnames and family names may drag us down, trap us, or they may unlock doors for us. Names and how we use them are important. If you are identified by a number in a prison or on an exam paper, you are depersonalized. Consider the names or titles you call yourself in your head. Do you have a sense of whose voice you are speaking in when you think of yourself with one name or another? Childhood nicknames can reassure us, or the long form can make us feel we are being told off. Do any of your names help you to be the person God calls you to be?

When Jesus met Peter, he told the fisherman called Simon that he now had another name, Peter, meaning a stone, pebble or rock. The reason for the choice, which emerged clearly later, was that Peter, who had proclaimed Jesus to be the Messiah, was to be the rock on which Jesus would build his Church. Other disciples had nicknames. James and John were 'the sons of thunder', presumably because they were noisy or argumentative. Rock revealed something about Peter's character that was already evident, but being renamed was also a call to develop certain aspects of himself. Rock was a name that Peter had to grow into and work with.

We find that Peter was a rock in a good and in a less good way. It is often our greatest gifts that, before they are mature, or when we go to the edges of them, trip us up and become our weaknesses. When we are good at conversation and making people feel at home, we may sometimes talk so much that we don't listen or people feel bombarded. When we are known as someone who helps others we may not take care of ourselves, which leads us to snap at people when we've had enough, and even to become resentful or ill.

Peter was to become the steady and firm place for others to find support as a chief pastor and a pillar of the Church. Peter didn't start out with these rock-like qualities, however. His name was a calling he had to grow into. As a new disciple he sank in the waves like a stone, was called a stumbling block by Jesus, and was unsupportive, falling asleep when Jesus needed him, not a rock on which Jesus could lean and rely.

You may want to sit lightly to your names. You may have names that draw you towards developing aspects of yourself after the example of a person or virtue expressed. In some cultures, parents give names that evoke qualities for the bearer to aspire to. Many names, often middle names, are virtues such as Grace, Patience or Victor, or family or saints' names such as Mary or John.

Might you choose a name that will help shape your life? There is much we can't change about our lives, particularly where we have come from, but also a great deal we can choose. Education enables you to choose new ancestors because what and who you study shapes your life just as the history of your family does. Many Christians down the ages have chosen a confirmation name of a saint who inspires them and found that the choice shapes them. At birth and baptism, names are given to us by others. The word 'christening', rather than 'baptism', has been remarkably persistent. Whatever the names we are given, being made Christ's as we are christened provides our identity as children of God and brothers and sisters in Christ.

- Call to mind your strengths and consider how they may sometimes trip you up. Are there weaknesses that have strengths within them that you haven't seen?
- Choose a name or quality to grow into.
- Do you have a godchild or someone you mentor whom you could pray for or be in touch with to support their growth?

Wednesday: be a bright flame before me

> Be a bright flame before me,
> a guiding star above me.
> Be a smooth path below me,
> a kindly shepherd behind me,
> today, tonight and for ever.
> (St Columba)

> The angel of the Lord appeared to [Moses] in a flame of fire out of a bush; he looked, and the bush was blazing, yet it was not consumed.
> (Exodus 3.2)

> Divided tongues, as of fire, appeared among them, and a tongue rested on each of them. (Acts 2.3)

As a new priest, I was taught that when you visit a sick person you should only stay for 20 minutes. Then, that didn't seem to me like giving someone their money's worth, especially if I'd paid for parking at the hospital. But I have long since realized, for myself as well as for others, that when people are ill or worried their concentration isn't at full capacity. There are other ways to express your care than staying for a long time, such as leaving fruit, or sending flowers or a card. I have also found that when ill or anxious it is hard to pray, to have the energy and concentration to string words together. So, it can be a source of strength knowing that others pray for you when you need prayer. I have found that short set prayers have enabled me to know God's presence in difficult times.

Some prayers – known as 'circle prayers' and associated particularly with the Celtic tradition – are written so that you can experience God surrounding you in times of vulnerability. Even if you can't remember the words, the image or picture presented in such prayers, often taken from the natural world, resonates with biblical stories and enables you to be open to God. One of my favourite circle prayers is the Prayer of St Columba, who lived in the sixth century on the Scottish island of Iona. The four images he uses are of the bright flame, guiding star, smooth path and kindly shepherd that surround the one praying in front, above, beneath and behind. The images connect with this desert territory that we have entered, but take us beyond it.

To imagine a bright flame before us recalls the story of the burning bush. Moses noticed the flames that signalled God's call on his life to play a part in freeing God's people from oppression. Moses had heard the stirrings of the call before, but got it wrong and had to flee. Others had heard it too, from before his birth. Many of them might seem unlikely participants in God's plan but, alert somehow to what God was doing, they joined in. They included the midwives Shiphrah and Puah who saved many Hebrew babies in Egypt by arriving late to the delivery room; an Egyptian princess who acted out of pity; Moses' mother, helped by her daughter Miriam, who hid her baby and was able to let him go to the river and to another woman in order that he might live (see Exodus 1 and 2). It was a priest of the Midian religion who mentored Moses, and gave him work and his daughter in marriage. Not all of these people knew the God of Israel, but they could sense the presence of God through their humanity, their own religion and the natural world. Sensing God's presence, they responded with wisdom, courage and compassion.

Moses was paying attention while working as a shepherd in the wilderness or desert of Midian. He noticed a bright flame, a bush that burned but didn't burn up. He was on holy ground, which was the path to freedom for God's people. Moses struggled with God the day he saw the burning bush, providing reasons and excuses why he couldn't go back to Egypt to plead for his people. He'd acted rashly and alone previously and murdered an Egyptian slave driver in anger. God answered every excuse, and the experience rekindled Moses' passion for the cause of freedom. Struggle often enables us to get in touch with what matters to us. That can involve a struggle with God, when something challenges us, and it makes us reconnect with earlier calls and passions. Moses experienced this rekindling and the clarity of God's guidance in fire. And it made sense: it was time to accept his past and not be held back by its failures.

Moses' early life had shaped him in such a way as to make him well placed to lead the Israelites from slavery to freedom, but he needed to come to terms with his personal history. He had been brought up in the royal courts. He spoke the language and knew the customs. He also knew he was different in race and religion, inferior in the eyes of those with power, and it made him angry. The desert was the place where Moses grew to a maturity, which enabled him to see the injustice and channel his anger in ways that meant he could be strategic, use his knowledge and skills, and work with others. He gained the respect of his fellow Israelites because he was of a family they knew, he worked with his brother and he had lived in the wilderness, the territory the people would have to cross to secure their freedom and resettle.

It is often those experiences of our lives that we would rather forget, or came by chance, which prove to be the making of us. Life comes in cycles, and if we can heal from hurts and the harmful effects of what has happened to us we can use the insights to go far and take others with us. Moses had 'been there', in Egypt and in the desert, and so he could return and lead others to a freedom that would be hard won.

The Prayer of St Columba invites God to be a bright flame in front of us. The burning bush showed Moses where God was, rekindled his desire to save his people and led him to take part in God's desire to free them. God will always lead us to love beyond ourselves. Fire is a symbol for God's presence in the story of the exodus. A circle prayer asks God to surround us with his presence. At Pentecost, the disciples experienced tongues of fire resting on them and the Holy Spirit dwelling in them. Those flames were both personal for each of them and, with the languages they spoke, a sign of God's blessing for all races and peoples. A flame before us draws our eyes to it, perhaps especially in the dark. God, a bright flame, draws us onwards, illuminating and warming our hearts.

- Are you aware of events or patterns in your life that you might ask for God's grace to be open about, to understand and to change?
- Perhaps there are passions or causes that you are now placed to rekindle and act on?
- Look for God's presence today. It will be in the call to human beings to love beyond themselves.

Thursday: be a guiding star above me

> For everything there is a season, and a time for every matter under heaven. (Ecclesiastes 3.1)

> Lead, kindly light, amid the encircling gloom,
> Lead thou me on;
> The night is dark, and I am far from home,
> Lead thou me on.
> Keep thou my feet; I do not ask to see
> The distant scene; one step enough for me.
> (John Henry Newman, 1801–90)

Alone in the darkness of the desert evenings, I longed for a shining star. The sun goes down at about six in the evening but the light of the stars and moon are not visible until closer to ten o'clock. If you are solitary, as I was, with no campfire or companions, the darkness can be terrifying, disorientating and lonely. A shining star brings light to see by, and it acts as a compass as well as a comfort. It is easy to see why the symbol of Islam, a faith forged in the desert, is a crescent moon and a star.

Although we think of the desert as unchanging through the centuries, over a 24-hour period there are dramatic changes of temperature, related of course to darkness and light. These constant changes within the changelessness taught me much about my ability to cope with fear and discomfort, and even to learn a bit about perseverance and hope.

The intensity of the heat during the day meant I was so hot and weary that I thought I would never be cool again. Then all of a sudden it got dark very quickly; I couldn't see a thing and began to feel cold. That was the most frightening time for me – the sunset until the time when I could see the moon and the stars. Then I could see by their light. It was not only the dark that was scary but also the cold. Having thought I would never be cool, at night I thought I would never be warm again.

After a day or so, I realized that this pattern was predictable. I don't mean the night and day, sun and moon, though of course that was predictable too. I mean that my fear and my belief that it would always be hot and I'd never again feel cold, or the other way round, was predictable. Remembering that I had had these fears before, I realized my belief that I would never be cool again was misplaced. I learned to trust the rhythms of the desert and to hold on, not lose hope, but extend my patience and endurance. The guiding of the star for me was learning that my ability to remember, to look up and just a little ahead, could engender trust so that just when it felt I could lose hope, the next cycle would begin.

In times of difficulty we think that nothing will change and we can't change anything. There are two things to consider: the changes that occur within ourselves –our internal choices – and our ability to live with the cycles of change. In 1945 Viktor Frankl, a Holocaust survivor and psychiatrist, wrote the classic text on resilience, *Man's Search for Meaning* (Random House, 2013). He describes the brutality of the concentration camp where people were dependent on the moods of the guards and treated as if they were animals. He observed that it was a rich inner life rather than physical hardiness that enabled people to live longer. Prisoners who were able to go through the huts comforting others, Frankl remarks, offered proof that everything can be taken from a person 'but one thing: the last of human freedoms – to choose one's attitude in any given set of circumstances, to choose one's own way'. Frankl was strengthened to choose how to respond to his situation by calling to mind the image of his wife and holding on to his humanity and spiritual freedom. What each prisoner needed to learn, he said, was that 'it did not really matter what we expected from life, but rather what life expected from us'. It may be action that is required, contemplation or to accept fate, but suffering has to be accepted as the task of a person's life, the unique opportunity lying in the way in which the burden is borne.

Understanding and learning to live with cycles of change is considered to be a sign of maturity. It is called 'seasonality'. When we have lived through the seasons many times, we are better able to recognize that there are seasons in life and its events: winter follows summer, just as spring follows winter. We can see there is a time for planting and a time for harvesting when we are involved in an organization. We can recognize the times when our ideas, offers of help or critique will be most helpful or welcome, and when not. In our relationships, we can get better at not reacting to one difficult interaction and instead take a longer view and intervene at a time when someone can hear what we say.

Having a broader view of time and timeliness, this development of seasonality involves being able to live with uncertainty and also emotional pain, another mark of maturity. Enduring isn't avoidance of engaging with complex situations out of cowardice or a lack of care for ourselves or others. Those of us who prefer instant answers and solutions will find it harder to resist the pull to speak or act now rather than bide time until a suitable opportunity. There have been times when I have feared that leaving something unsaid would build resentment in me, or that I might forget to say anything and something would be lost. My experience is that a little time has enabled me to cling less to whatever the issue was and understand more how to proceed. I have found that when I have understood the situation more deeply and my part in it, life has presented me with an opportunity to express what I have wanted to.

As Christians, it is the journey of the Magi that may come to mind when we think about being guided by a star, though it isn't seasonal in Lent. The Magi, of course, read the stars since they were astronomers and astrologers rolled into one. They looked for the meaning in the heavens and, having discerned it, followed its guidance. Viktor Frankl found that suffering itself has meaning for us and if we use our spiritual freedom to meet its challenges we find that meaning.

In times of difficulty we have to trust, endure and exercise patience, for the time will pass and the challenge change, even go away altogether. Endurance isn't putting up with something, or gritting your teeth, but choosing to hold fast for a time, or in a particular way for that bit longer than seems possible. If we can look up in the darkness and notice when the first star appears we will find guidance, meaning and the blessing of light to lead us.

- What are the choices that you make, in which you express your spiritual freedom despite constrained circumstances?

Friday: be a smooth path beneath me

Lead us not into temptation.
(From the Lord's Prayer)

Enter through the narrow gate; for the gate is wide and the road is easy that leads to destruction, and there are many who take it. For the gate is narrow and the road is hard that leads to life, and there are few who find it. (Matthew 7.13–14)

Teenagers often experience being grounded. I don't mean being in touch with reality, but detained at home rather than being allowed to go out, as a punishment or consequence for some misdemeanour. Being grounded or sent to your room can start as a punishment but it can become a chance to be in touch with what is familiar and sustaining and so find some perspective and balance. You may remember the classic children's story by Maurice Sendak, written in 1963 but still popular: *Where the Wild Things Are* (Random House, 2000). A little boy, Max, has a tantrum. He is sent to his room but travels to a magical land of monsters, seemingly far away, but after a time the place gradually becomes his very own room where he finds that his supper is still hot.

Any difficulty confines us in some way, as does the territory of the desert, and so we experience being grounded, in touch with a reality we might not want and unable to go out. But we do not stand still and certainly don't want to become stagnant or static. We may need to stand our ground, but not dig in our heels or jump to conclusions. The prayer of St Columba forces us to think of movement by having not just ground but also a path beneath us.

Travelling along is made easier by a smooth path. Similarly, you get to a place more quickly if the path is straight, as John the Baptist recommended we make the path through our hearts to God. To ask God to be a smooth path reminds me of the words of the Lord's Prayer where we pray not to be led into temptation but to be delivered from evil. Struggle brings life, and the struggle to overcome temptation strengthens our resolve, but human beings are made for happiness. To pray that everything would come together for us, that the path may be smooth, opens us to the reality of God's grace and times of ease and joy.

Many of our struggles are the ordinary ones along life's path. Like a toddler in a tantrum we need a secure place to express our frustration at our situation and regain our composure. We need a non-judgemental helper to provide our supper. Temptation is the struggle when we already know which way is the right one and which the one that leads to destruction, but we are finding we are pulled in different directions. Jesus describes the two ways as the broad and narrow. Knowing the way of life is narrow, we pray for it to be smooth.

We can even out our own path by taking care of ourselves. Without self-care, we trip up and fall down unnecessarily. When we clear the path in front of our own house it means that the way is easier for others too. We don't help ourselves or others if we don't take time off. Our way can be made smooth when we deliberately rest from the current struggle, put it aside in some way. Distractions can give our minds a rest, and going away relieves our bodies too.

We imagine that the monks and nuns who lived in the desert never let up, but there are many warnings about the dangers of not letting up, not least the danger of pride:

> A hunter in the desert saw Abba Anthony enjoying himself with the brethren and he was shocked. Wanting to show him that it was necessary sometimes to meet the needs of the brethren the old man said to him, 'Put an arrow in your bow and shoot it.' So he did. The old man then said, 'Shoot another', and he did so. Then the old man said, 'Shoot yet again', and the hunter replied, 'If I bend my bow so much I will break it.' Then the old man said to him, 'It is the same with the work of God. If we stretch the brethren beyond measure they will soon break. Sometimes it is necessary to come down to meet their needs.' When he heard his words the hunter was pierced with compunction and, greatly edified by the old man, he went away. As for the brethren, they went home strengthened. (Anthony 13)

If a path is smooth you can look up and look around you. You can look into the faces of those you travel with. If a path is stony and difficult you find yourself looking at your feet, though very grateful if someone else can reach out with a hand from a more secure footing and provide support. Those helpers are like the angels who ministered to Jesus in his 40 days in the desert.

Taking care to make a path smooth as well as straight is a gift we offer ourselves out of self-respect and an awareness of our situation. It is a gift we can also offer to others, by being gentle in our words, listening carefully and creating a space for someone else, by denial of our own priorities for the sake of someone else's need. Self-denial is a Lenten virtue and one to be employed for the sake of another. Love is the first principle for a Christian. St John Cassian, in writing about fasting, describes the way in which a monk who is undergoing a fast of several weeks denies himself this chance to grow spiritually for the sake of love: if someone comes to visit the monk, Cassian states that he should cook a meal and sit down to eat with that person. Hospitality to a neighbour is more important than personal piety.

The Christian way of life is a narrow way with many ups and downs, difficulties, and the temptation then to stand still or turn back, or go off the path. The prayer for a smooth path helps us to be thankful for the ways in which the journey of our lives has been smooth and keeps us humble as we recognize, when we see others struggle, that 'There, but for the grace of God, go I.'

- As you ask God to make your path smooth, consider how you might be an instrument of your own prayer by being gentle with yourself and with any others you can see are struggling in some way to find a firm path.
- Many churches, like other public buildings, have become more alert to making a smooth path for those who cannot walk and use wheelchairs, prams or pushchairs by having ramps made, or signage and hospitality to help people feel welcomed. Do the organizations you are involved in make paths smooth?

Saturday: be a kindly shepherd behind me

Surely goodness and mercy shall follow me
all the days of my life,
and I shall dwell in the house of the LORD
my whole life long. (Psalm 23.6)

I am the good shepherd.
(John 10.11)

It isn't always a nice experience having someone behind us. I get rather frustrated when I can sense someone standing behind me, in a supermarket perhaps, someone who doesn't make themselves or their needs known. 'Excuse me' would do very nicely and I'd be happy to move. If I don't sense someone behind me and then he or she speaks, I'm likely to exclaim, 'Oh, you made me jump!' The shepherd in the Prayer of St Columba is kindly. We are not in his way and he doesn't want to make us jump. The kindly shepherd watches our backs so that we are protected, he provides a steadying hand, and from time to time he may even give us a helpful prod in the right direction. Though we think of discipleship as following, here we can be assured that goodness and mercy follow us.

The image of the kindly shepherd resonates with the best-known and most often sung psalm, the twenty-third. There the shepherd is the Lord who leads his sheep to lie down, to rest, to be replenished by still waters and green grass. While the sheep feed and rest, the shepherd watches over them. Seeing somewhere beautiful, eating properly, being looked after and sleeping are all vital for us at any time, but particularly if we are low or in a valley in our life. These are times when fears can arise and we can feel panicky, weary and anxious. We can notice these feelings by the way in which we sigh or find ourselves breathing quickly. Once we feel safe, it is much easier for us to take some rest, be calm and be restored.

In Psalm 23 the shepherd is depicted as ahead, but the kindly shepherd is behind us and would have us look back. Behind us lies all that is past, and the kindly shepherd turns us round from time to time to look at the past. There is generally much to let go of and be released from our personal history. When we look back we need to do so from a place of safety. With a kindly shepherd, we might be able to look at our younger or more vulnerable or foolish selves through his eyes of love and with a kindness that doesn't crush us but allows us to take the path to freedom. The shepherd looks on our past with love, forgiveness and healing, and as he turns us round he holds us to enable us to look and remember knowing all that he, as the Good Shepherd, has accomplished.

When people are behind us we can find we have to wait for them because we've forged ahead. We can keep looking back just in case they've disappeared. The ability to wait on God is a sign of maturing faith. When we add up the four weeks of Advent, the six weeks of Lent and the ten days between Ascension and Pentecost when the disciples waited for the gift of the Holy Spirit, we find that the invitation to wait takes up almost a quarter of the Church's year. We can mirror what waiting on God involves by listening to our breathing.

Though we can control our breathing to some extent, we might more accurately say that our bodies are breathed, rather than we breathe. Our body breathes even when we are not aware of it. Take a breath and when you breathe out keep breathing, right to the end of the breath, and let yourself feel the sensation of your chest moving in order for your lungs to draw the next breath in. Breathing in starts very deep down in our bodies, long before the breath rushes in. There is a pause between breathing in and the next breath out, and also between the out-breath and the next in-breath. The pause between breaths happens continually and our body waits for the next move each time. This waiting isn't like waiting in a queue. Like the waiting in the Church's year, in Advent it is expectant of new life; in Lent it is the body preparing for what is to come; in the ten days between Ascension and Pentecost it involves staying put and praying with others.

We don't always find it easy to wait for the next thing to happen. If we are impatient we are inclined to rush on from one thing to another, not stopping to savour, to pause, or to look back and take in more deeply what we have done, heard or experienced. Rest or pausing is important in the in-between times, or times of transition, which are vulnerable times in our lives. Our bodies are familiar with these times of pausing as we breathe, and we could learn from them. Noticing our breathing allows us to be in touch with who we are and open to the creativity of God in the pause. Our bodies prepare themselves for each new breath. Each breath pledges us again to our lives, to the world, and it also provides the energy to live.

- Develop a sense of the kindly shepherd behind you, one who watches your back, holds your past and prompts you forward in such a way that you know you will be provided for in all that awaits.
- Read Psalm 23 with the sense of this kindly shepherd behind you. Might you look back and wait on God?
- Spend some time noticing the pause between your inhalation and exhalation.

FLOURISH: THE SECOND WEEK

> He makes me lie down in green pastures;
> he leads me beside still waters;
> he restores my soul. (Psalm 23.2–3)
>
> I shall dwell in the house of the Lord
> my whole life long. (Psalm 23.6)

God's desire is that we flourish, living life to the full. Jesus said, 'I came that they may have life, and have it abundantly' (John 10.10). Living fully and deeply as a human being includes the experience of suffering and pain. Our society tends towards thinking that there must be something wrong in this, that it isn't natural or normal to experience difficulty or sadness. Sometimes Christians can join in with this and think that Christian faith is an insurance policy against things being difficult. Alternatively, there are those who seem to relish a certain misery or martyr-like demeanour, imagining it is related to holiness.

When we experience adversity, we have to get through it and cope. Then we rebuild our lives so that we can flourish. Sometimes, if we are to move on fully, we need to let go of the habits we forged when the need was simply to survive, and replace them with new habits and freedoms. Just like coping, flourishing relates to our external circumstances but most importantly to our inner life. As we rebuild our lives and heal we build a house where we have shelter and are protected. When we are more secure we can be more accepting and at home in ourselves. Flourishing involves making an inner home in which we can dwell and find inner peace. To do this still involves careful discipline, including setting boundaries, but not barriers, for ourselves and other people. It involves honing and using our strengths. The wisdom of the desert Christians of the fourth and fifth centuries points us to the importance of attending to and protecting our inner life, to not judging ourselves or others. Jesus advises us to let our peace return to us when we experience rejection and to dwell in him.

Prayers for the week

For the morning

New every morning is the love
Our wakening and uprising prove;
Through sleep and darkness safely brought,
Restored to life and power and thought.

New mercies, each returning day,
Hover around us while we pray;
New perils past, new sins forgiven,
New thoughts of God, new hopes of heaven.

If on our daily course our mind
Be set to hallow all we find,
New treasures still, of countless price,
God will provide for sacrifice.

The trivial round, the common task,
Will furnish all we need to ask,
Room to deny ourselves, a road
To bring us daily nearer God.

Only, O Lord, in Thy dear love
Fit us for perfect rest above;
And help us, this and every day,
To live more nearly as we pray.
(John Keble, 1792–1866)

For the evening

Glory to Thee, my God, this night,
For all the blessings of the light;
Keep me, O keep me, King of kings,
Beneath Thine own almighty wings.

Forgive me, Lord, for Thy dear Son,
The ill that I this day have done,
That with the world, myself, and Thee,
I, ere I sleep, at peace may be.

Teach me to live, that I may dread
The grave as little as my bed;
Teach me to die, that so I may
Rise glorious at the aweful day.

O may my soul on Thee repose,
And with sweet sleep mine eyelids close;
Sleep that may me more vigorous make,
To serve my God when I awake.

Praise God from whom all blessings flow,
Praise Him, all creatures here below,
Praise Him above, ye heavenly host,
Praise Father, Son, and Holy Ghost.
(Thomas Ken, 1637–1711)

Circle prayer

Circle me, O Lord, with your loving presence,
Keep fear without and calm within,
Keep fear without and hope within,
Keep fear without and love within,
This day and always.

Traditional Gaelic blessing

May the road rise up to meet you.
May the wind be always at your back.
May the sun shine warm upon your face,
the rains fall soft upon your fields and, until we meet again,
may God hold you in the palm of his hand.

Words from Scripture

Take heart, it is I; do not be afraid. (Matthew 14.27)

You desire truth in the inward being;
therefore teach me wisdom in my secret heart.
(Psalm 51.6)

A psalm to read

Psalm 62

Monday: build a house

> Everyone then who hears these words of mine and does them will be like a wise man who built his house on the rock. The rain fell, the floods came, and the winds blew and beat on that house, but it did not fall, because it had been founded on rock. (Matthew 7.24–25)

When adversity strikes, we have to build our lives again, and Construct, the third C after Coping and Constancy describing resilience. The rains will come down and the floods will come up in any of our lives, but if we have built our house on rock we will withstand them. If we have built on sand we will collapse and sometimes we have done exactly that, perhaps due to less than stable parenting, for example. We've had to build on sand and it hasn't enabled good foundations to be dug, nor has it provided a surface for any kind of weight bearing. Rock, however, is firm, solid and dependable, having stood the test of time. In the experiences of adversity, we have to look for the rock amid all the sand and build our lives again.

Frank Lake, a Christian psychiatrist, was one of the pioneers of the Pastoral Counselling Movement in the 1960s. Many Christian priests and pastors learned from the Clinical Theology Association that Lake founded. Drawing on human development theory, they learned about the healing of troubled minds and memories. Erik Erikson, a developmental psychologist (1902–94), had set out eight stages of life. We grow through life, he taught, not just by our physical growth and decline, but because of the way in which we come through the inner conflicts we face as we mature and the relationships we have. Lake used the image of a chair to describe how our personalities are forged. He called it the Chair of Identity. The four legs of the chair are foundational and relate to the ways in which we have learned to trust, develop autonomy, initiate action and be industrious. If we don't secure these well enough we can find it difficult to trust people; we doubt ourselves, feel shame, guilt and inferiority. The seat of the chair is our identity; as we grow securely into young adults, when it is firm enough we can lean back and invite another into a loving relationship.

Throughout our lives we continue to develop and heal and our chair gets reshaped. We don't start again, and we are always shaped with the early materials we had to work with. Lake's chair of identity always reminds me of one of Michael Bond's stories about Paddington Bear. Paddington attempts to mend a wobbly table by sawing off a bit of one leg, but he saws off a bit too much of several legs, several times, and ends up with something reshaped and a lot lower than it was. Paddington doesn't ask for help – he cuts off and casts away and ends up with rather a low table. The Brown family, of course, help him out and all is well. We are like that lovable bear, getting into scrapes, but finding there is love, help and grace at hand, in God and from God's people. Much about us is already in place but we develop through life and we are reshaped. The house that is our life can always be redesigned, with rooms used differently perhaps, so that we become a place where we can be at home and hospitable.

If you imagine a child's drawing of a house you will have the roof and walls, doors, windows, and perhaps a fence and gate. These give you protection and shelter, a way in and the chance to see out. Some of us find it is or has been difficult to say no to the demands of others and have had to learn to set boundaries. Without them we can be overstretched and unable to meet the demands we're committed to, or we compromise our well-being, not for any great cause, but because we haven't taken into account our humanity. In times of adversity remaining Constant, as well as Coping and Constructing, is important in order to be resilient. Resisting the forces of destruction by setting boundaries helps us to be constant in who we are and what we seek. Boundaries prevent continual low-level internal disputes about borders, expectations and territory. It is important to be able to shut your door and to be responsible for mowing the lawn on your side of the fence only. A boundary isn't a barrier, however. Doors can also be opened and fences are places to lean over and chat. We put boundaries around time as well as space by establishing routines or marking time off in our diaries. Planning ahead in time and space can seem time-consuming and uncreative, but it can provide what we need to live well and love well.

Holman Hunt, in 1854, painted the very famous picture of Jesus as the Light of the World. It's inspired by a verse from the book of Revelation: 'Listen! I am standing at the door, knocking; if you hear my voice and open the door, I will come in to you and eat with you, and you with me' (3.20). Whenever the picture was mentioned my mother always used to remind whoever was listening that if we looked carefully we would see that there is no door handle on the outside of the door. Jesus doesn't barge in, but knocks. We have to listen for the knock and we have to open the door. I have always found the image of Jesus knocking, wanting to come in to have supper, reassuring in its portrayal of Christ as insistent yet respectful, waiting and wanting to stay a while. Jesus is perfectly happy at the kitchen table.

As we grow in wisdom we build our house, our life, in such a way that we can be open to Christ who knocks and, bringing his light, sits and eats with us. We rearrange furniture and redecorate all the time, creating space and redefining boundaries so that we can dwell in peace and be open and welcoming to others.

- You might like to consider what you value most when you are a guest in someone else's space and how you might make others feel valued, by your words, actions or the space you offer for them at home or at work.
- How might you this week invest in your space in some way so that it enables you to live well and flourish? You may like to choose a Bible verse or saying that helps you know God is near you in this desert territory. You could record it in some way, perhaps on a sticky note, a blackboard or a screen, if sewing a tapestry is a step too far.
- Are there boundaries for you to set and keep?

Tuesday: take heart

> When you pass through the waters, I will be with you;
> and through the rivers, they shall not overwhelm you;
> when you walk through fire you shall not be burned,
> and the flame shall not consume you. (Isaiah 43.2)

> He said not, thou shalt not be tempested, thou shalt not be travailed, thou shalt not be afflicted. He said, Thou shalt not be overcome.
> (Mother Julian of Norwich)

I enjoy interviewing people for jobs, as volunteers or for a paid role. I'm fascinated by the ways in which people end up where they are via unexpected routes and the interesting experiences they've had along the way. The best outcome is to find a person who fits the role in such a way that they flourish – their strengths are used to the full and they continue to develop. Being interviewed, though, is pretty demanding, however friendly the members of the panel are. Often there are various tests, from psychological profiling to typing, from presentations to trial by canapé – the latter performed within the whirl of social chit-chat while precariously balancing a glass and a plate.

The story of the night when Peter walks on water (Matthew 14.22–33) reads to me like three rounds of an interview process for the position of lead disciple. It's as nail-bitingly tense as the TV show *The Apprentice*, and Peter gets to the last round. Later on Jesus tells them all that it is Peter who is the rock on which he will build his church.

The first round of the leadership contest that was held that night on Lake Galilee was the storm, the second was the sighting of what the disciples think is a ghost, and then the third, the walking on the water. Each round had the disciples in difficult situations and tested their ability to face fear. Leaning in rather than pulling away from difficulty and fear is vital if we are to overcome. As Nelson Mandela said, 'I learned that courage was not the absence of fear, but the triumph over it.'

That night Jesus' disciples sailed across the lake and encountered a storm in which the wind was against them and the waves battered the boat. It's a tough situation, but a common one for a boat sailing across Lake Galilee. Quite a few of the disciples were skilled fishermen and we don't have a sense that they were unduly worried, certainly not terrified, even though it was a rough night. Some of them trusted those who could sail to get them through the storm; they would have needed to take their advice on how to help and when to keep out of the way. They worked as a group, drawing on the skills that were needed for that situation.

The first round of the discipleship contest was about coping, facing the storms of life using your own skills and resources and those of your fellow disciples. What terrified the disciples was seeing a shadowy figure coming towards them from across the lake. They thought it was a ghost. Life at sea has always led sailors the world over to develop stories of mysterious creatures, for example sirens who would lure them to their death. A ghost might represent some malign presence to hurt them, or someone from beyond the grave to tell them that death is near, or some guilty secret come to claim revenge. The fear of the ghost is within them. It is internal, and paralysing, and if not overcome would prevent them from managing the boat safely.

The second round of the contest is managing fear. Our fears can increase, get out of control and lead to panic in uncertain and dangerous situations, and that can take us by surprise if we generally cope with life. Recognizing fear is the first step towards overcoming it. Facing fear or leaning in to it is the second step. The disciples cry out and they get a response from Jesus. 'Take heart,' he says, 'it is I; do not be afraid.' Where they were terrified, they find Jesus reassuring them, directing them to take heart. The picture of discipleship in this story is not passive. The disciples manage the storm with their own resources, and in fear of a ghost they are invited to recognize the presence of Jesus and take heart. They have to find their courage.

In round three of this discipleship contest Peter has enough courage to turn the tables on Jesus and test him out. You know how in a job interview you are told that you are interviewing the bosses as much as they are interviewing you, and although that is true, it doesn't really feel quite like that? Peter decides to test this ghost – is it really Jesus, and if it is, what kind of teacher and miracle-worker walks on water? Might these powers extend to him too? Peter, having gathered his courage, takes a risk. 'Lord, if it is you, command me to come to you on the water,' he asks. We should be careful what we ask God for, for Jesus says, 'Come.'

We know what happens and I expect a superficial assessment is that Peter fails. He sinks and has to be rescued. I wonder if we might think rather that Peter shows real trust in Jesus and the makings of a spiritual leader. He gets out of the boat and walks on the water, trusting in Jesus. He is overcome by fear as the waves touch him, and so he is pulled down and overwhelmed. So he calls out to Jesus who immediately grasps him. So often when I have read this story I have thought that Peter had failed, that the words 'You of little faith, why did you doubt?' are so much more important than the word 'Come' or 'Take heart, it is I; do not fear.' Peter's trust in Jesus failed him so that he couldn't continue to walk on water, but it was strong enough for him to know Jesus could save him from drowning.

Peter gets to round three of the discipleship contest and emerges as best placed to be the leader. That's not because he can or can't walk on water. Peter can lead because he uses his own skill and courage. He can risk failure for the chance of something great. He takes heart from Jesus' presence, follows his direction and is not too proud to know when he needs saving.

- What challenges you to grow in developing your strengths?
- Pray a circle prayer (see pages 27, 29 and 42) to secure it in your memory for times of fear.
- Can you, by words of encouragement, seek to overturn a judgement of someone that has left that person with a sense of persistent failure?

Wednesday: guard your inner life

> Like a city breached, without walls, is one who lacks self-control.
> (Proverbs 25.28)

> Do not judge so that you may not be judged. For with the judgement you make you will be judged, and the measure you give will be the measure you get. (Matthew 7.1–2)

We have become increasingly aware of the need for physical exercise and more aware of the way in which physical exercise supports our mental health in various ways, such as the sense of achievement it brings, the social connections and being out in the fresh air. When we are conscious of our bodies working hard, we are forced to consider their needs. That also happens through physical illness. Being aware of our bodies, their strengths and weaknesses, drives us inwards and invites us to attend to what's important, our priorities and our spiritual life.

The traditional religious and spiritual discipline that forces us inward is fasting. Fasting is common in our society but as Christians we don't often relate it to spiritual discipline. A fast is where we decide to avoid some food or drink for a certain period of time in order to gain or restore well-being in some aspect of our lives, physical, emotional, mental or spiritual. Detoxing, and adopting a low-cholesterol, vegan or gluten-free diet, are examples of practices that will enable us to gain or restore health. Many people give something up for Lent, recognizing the value of such self-discipline, sometimes for a sense of personal achievement or the good of the environment, at other times to be in solidarity with the poor or a family member on a restricted diet. You may have chosen to give something up for Lent or have had to change your diet for your well-being.

Fasting helps to regain energy levels, orientation and purpose. The self-control we need to do it has us questioning ourselves when it gets tough, about the purpose of doing it, whether it or we are worth it. We ponder quite *why* it is so difficult to keep a fast. I have found that when I have fasted during the day I have had to learn not to be irritable with others in the late afternoon and early evening just because I haven't eaten, since others should not have to suffer because of a choice I have made. It has given me increased respect for those in our world who eat only once a day due to poverty. Fasting has perhaps even enabled me to express my irritation less, having learned to recognize it and lay it aside when hungry and so generally become more patient with myself and other people.

When our bodies make demands on us and we have to give them attention, we are drawn to live more holistically because our mind, will, emotions and spirit become engaged. This can be forced on us, our own choice or a by-product of something else. The desert Christians fasted in order to grow spiritually and in order to guard their inner lives. A strong inner life is vital to enable people to come through adversity well, and spiritual practices like fasting, prayer and reading Scripture, all recommended during Lent, resource our inner lives.

It is from within that we are able to meet the challenges of life. The call to guard our inner lives is in order to focus our strength and energy on healing and growth and it is a call that requires self-discipline. In the studies of what qualities are seen in those who are resilient, self-discipline is core. A practice such as fasting is not encouraging navel-gazing, but enabling openness to God so that we might grow in wisdom and compassion from a place of integration within us. The monastic tradition describes this openness as 'purity of heart'. Our inner lives need to be healed from the fragmentation caused by life's experiences, sin and fear. By guarding our inner life through self-discipline, we make a straight path to God.

It takes energy to heal from our hurts and we can waste energy if we don't guard our inner life. A key way to guard our inner life is by not wasting energy in judging others and ourselves. Self-blame is very destructive to our mental and emotional health and constantly comparing ourselves to others and being judgemental is highly destructive. Judging prevents us from being at peace. Non-judgement is a constant theme of the desert Christians, perhaps because if we seek to improve we can easily rate ourselves against others in a way that is counterproductive. One of the Sayings of the desert Christians emphasizes this:

> Abba Poemen said that Abba Paphnutius used to say, 'During the whole lifetime of the old men, I used to go and see them twice a month, although it was a distance of twelve miles. I told them each of

> my thoughts and they never answered me anything but this, "wherever you go, do not judge yourself and you will be at peace."'
>
> (Paphnutius 3)

Another Saying recommends a method to help when we are inclined to use up energy in blaming and judging:

> Abba Anoub asked Abba Poemen about the impure thoughts which the heart of man brings forth and about vain desires. Abba Poeman said to him, 'Is the axe any use without someone to cut with it? (Isaiah 10:15) If you do not make use of these thoughts, they will be ineffectual too.'
>
> (Poemen 15)

It can be very difficult to stop going over things in our minds. The desert Christians taught a mental self-discipline that involved cutting dead destructive thoughts when they come to mind and replacing them with repeated words from Scripture. They recognized that we follow trains of thought, *logosmoi*, and we need to be alert to where they lead. Perhaps we can think of it as knowing when to get out of the carriage of a train of thought. We learn because so many times previously the train of thought has carried us crashing into the buffers. We will need to spend some days noticing our trains of thought and if there are some that we need to be disciplined about stopping. Abba Poemen says we need to take an axe to some thoughts. As we do this we should have ready some phrase from the Bible, some words of Jesus, or lyric from a song, with which to begin a new train of thought. Whatever we choose will direct us in a way that is pure, in that it uses our attention and energy for healing, love and life. Destructive thoughts from our past or from our day do not need to drive us. Remember, the axe cuts off the energy that fuels a cycle of pointless rumination. It isn't a spade that would bury thoughts we need to deal with, for then the thoughts fester and return in another form.

- If you have given up something for Lent, consider how the practice is directing your train of thought. If you haven't, perhaps fast for a day, or give something up for one of the weeks of Lent, and be attentive to what it teaches you.
- Are there trains of thought that you know have you straying into 'impure thoughts' – ones that take you to rumination and self-blame rather than to truth, beauty, hope, love, to God?

Thursday: the reality of suffering

> If you continue in my word, you are truly my disciples . . . and the truth will make you free. (John 8.31–32)

> From that time on, Jesus began to show his disciples that he must go to Jerusalem and undergo great suffering at the hands of the elders and chief priests and scribes, and be killed, and on the third day be raised. And Peter took him aside and began to rebuke him, saying, 'God forbid it, Lord! This must never happen to you.' But he turned and said to Peter, 'Get behind me, Satan! You are a stumbling-block to me; for you are setting your mind not on divine things but on human things.' Then Jesus told his disciples, 'If any want to become my followers, let them deny themselves and take up their cross and follow me. For those who want to save their life will lose it, and those who lose their life for my sake will find it.' (Matthew 16.21–25)

In 2013 the chief operating officer of Facebook, Sheryl Sandberg, published a book, titled *Lean In: Women, work and the will to lead* (Random House). The book is an international bestseller and Sandberg shares what she has learned as a highly successful businesswoman.

However, later in 2015 Sandberg suffered a personal tragedy. Her husband and the father of her two young children died very suddenly, aged 47. Her life fell apart and she learned a great deal about what it takes to come through and support others in suffering. In 2017 she wrote another book to share those insights: *Option B: Facing adversity, building resilience, and finding joy* (Random House).

Before her personal tragedy, Sandberg had said to a friend diagnosed with cancer, 'I know you are going to be all right.' She now knows that was crass and so she says, 'I don't know whether it'll be all right or not, but I will be with you as you go through this every step of the way.' Sandberg, as a highly successful entrepreneur, didn't have much experience of suffering or insight into its place in the fabric of human life. We might say its *vital* place, because it is through loss and struggle that, when we look back, many of us realize we have gained maturity and even a little wisdom.

Peter wasn't prepared to accept that the person he looked up to, learned from and knew was God's anointed would ever have to suffer: 'God forbid it, Lord! This must never happen to you.' Peter seemed to expect that the crowds and the miracles would result in glory and success. For Jesus, and for other great leaders, there is struggle and suffering, particularly at the point at which they begin to challenge injustice or others become jealous of their influence. Jesus was clear that his call involved suffering. Peter cared about Jesus and didn't want to face the possibility of him making the ultimate sacrifice. He wanted to help, and to prevent anything bad happening. It is natural to want to protect those we care about. To see one's loved ones – children in particular – in pain is very hard to bear. It's to do with our empathy and compassion, certainly, as well our sense that we should be able to ease or stop the pain, as we could soothe a bad dream or a grazed knee.

Neither current success nor love can prevent tragedy happening, and if we pretend it can, we become less able to face it when it happens and less trustworthy to our friends. 'Get behind me, Satan!' must have been difficult words for Peter to hear. Jesus pushes Peter away because he struggled to face the inevitable rejection and suffering that he would experience. He needed Peter to be truthful and supportive in the suffering and not pretend there wouldn't be any.

When we suffer, we need people to be with us who do not deny that we are in pain, worried, uncertain about how we will cope or what the future holds. We need truth, and as Jesus said, 'The truth will make you free.' That's what Sheryl Sandberg learned from those who helped her through the early stage of grief and what she now offers to friends when they suffer.

'Deny yourself, take up your cross, and follow me' isn't a post that's going to have lots of likes on Facebook, but it is the path on which we must travel to bring about life and growth. Taking up your cross is public solidarity with those about to die, those cast out and those who have done wrong. As we experience suffering we find our hearts more open to those who stumble, or are down on their luck or incapacitated.

Denying yourself can only come when you have a sense of self, and a self that can lay aside self-interest to bring about good. That can involve stopping ourselves from needing to express our opinion or having the last word. It can be going without sometimes to give to someone in need, or just to bring them joy. It can be accepting the struggle that will mean we grow more mature, and not avoiding it.

'Deny yourself, take up your cross and follow me.' Peter doesn't cease to try to be a hero, but he continues to follow Christ. He becomes more of a rock and less of a stumbling block. There are times of suffering and setbacks in all our lives, times when these open us up to God, to others, and we end up strangely grateful for them, or aspects of them. We find we have lost some things but gained others.

Suffering is not failure; neither is getting it wrong, for Peter or for us. The only failure for Christians is a lack of love. We don't learn the lessons of discipleship all at once and often need to learn the same lesson twice. But we keep responding to Christ's call: 'Follow me.'

- Has suffering enabled you to offer compassion more effectively to someone else? Can you use this learning again this week?
- Pray for someone who is suffering.

Friday: wipe the dust from your feet

As you enter the house, greet it. If the house is worthy, let your peace come upon it; but if it is not worthy, let your peace return to you. If anyone will not welcome you or listen to your words, shake off the dust from your feet as you leave that house or town. (Matthew 10.12–14)

He makes me lie down in green pastures;
he leads me beside still waters;
he restores my soul. (Psalm 23.2–3)

When our family was on holiday, when I was a child, I really loved being able to go to someone's house as part of the trip, perhaps to visit an elderly aunt or some friends my parents hadn't seen for a while. While the adults chatted I realized I could get to know about the people whose home it was just by being in their space. Some were very precious about their ornaments and wouldn't let children into some rooms. There were people who made sure we wiped our feet carefully on the mat, and those who insisted that we took our shoes off at the door.

You can enter someone's home or room and not feel welcomed in obvious and subtle ways. When we are told to get out or not invited to a gathering, we know we are being rejected. When someone talks over us, or doesn't listen or give us their attention, we know they do not want to hear us. There are times when we brush this off as insignificant or not what someone usually does and so we give him or her the benefit of the doubt. At other times we have to take notice of it because it changes something about our lives and our relationship with a community, family or individual. Sometimes this experience hurts more because we are vulnerable just now or it has happened before and so we remember that pain too. We are hurt by rejection, criticism or gossip that has reached our ears and this experience invades our personal space, not necessarily physically, but our mental or heart space in some way, diminishing us.

Growing in resilience involves being more robust and discerning when we are not welcomed or accepted. Abba Poemen said, 'If I am in a place where there are enemies, I become a soldier' (Poemen 202). Although we may be conscious, especially in Lent, of the call of Jesus to deny ourselves, we cannot deny our self without a sense of self. Self-esteem gets knocked when we experience adversity and we have to draw on our inner resources. Our self-esteem may not have been very strong throughout our lives. We become more able to withstand adversity, that is, we can grow more resilient, by focusing on our inner life and our sense of self. When we are low or don't have much confidence, we are likely to feel keenly any snub and shrink a little.

Jesus tells his disciples to go out and tell people the good news of God's love, and he gives advice about what to do when no one listens and it's clear they aren't welcome. 'Shake or wipe the dust from your feet and let your peace return to you,' he tells them. When we have been rejected in some way it is natural to feel cross and so we will probably start by turning our backs on the experience, perhaps shrugging our shoulders, perhaps feeling outraged, sometimes – if we are low – secretly thinking people are right to reject us. Shaking their dust and that experience off our feet vigorously ensures we recognize the hurt and don't pretend this hasn't happened. To grow resilient through this, though, requires us to focus on our inner selves, initially to recover, steady ourselves and care for ourselves. As we carefully wipe the dust from our feet we can let go. When we are gentle with our feet and take time to refresh them, it helps us to walk in a different direction. When we feel attacked it is easy to attack back and be defensive. Jesus doesn't recommend a clever answer or action at the point of rejection. He tells us to let our peace return to us.

God tells Moses, in the desert, to take off his shoes because he stands in the presence of God, on holy ground (Exodus 3.5). Each of us, made in the image of God, has an innate dignity, and to become who we truly are, we have to stand, with the grace of God, in our own stead, claiming our presence. This isn't the same as standing on our own two feet. In the face of rejection, it is being able to stand our ground rather than dig in our heels. It is letting our peace return to us.

When I was a child our house felt empty and cold if my mother was not in. She had a huge presence that, although at times I found it overwhelming and even invasive, I generally experienced as warm and energetic. We all have a presence and as we mature as people and in Christ our inner life grows stronger and more palpable to others. It takes courage to be able to say, calmly and from a place of inner peace, that you would rather someone didn't speak in such a way to you, or that you were hurt by something, or that you wish to say sorry. To say such a thing builds your inner life and sense of self and is fuelled from time in prayer and time resting. It comes from experiencing the shepherd leading us to still waters so that he can restore our soul.

Your inner peace isn't passive, but active. It is your life-force. When you meet someone or go to a person's home, as Jesus describes, you convey your self and your peace rests there, on them. Peace isn't static, but dynamic. The Gaelic blessing, 'Deep peace of the running wave to you', set to music by John Rutter, recognizes the inner movement and flexibility we need to be at peace and be peacemakers. To feel at home is to experience inner peace, a peace that will be expressed as a gift and the blessing of your presence.

- Hear this prayer of blessing for yourself and seek to live from that peace:

> Deep peace of the running wave to you.
> Deep peace of the flowing air to you.
> Deep peace of the quiet earth to you.
> Deep peace of the shining stars to you.
> Deep peace of the gentle night to you.
> Moon and stars pour their healing light on you.
> Deep peace of Christ,
> of Christ the light of the world, to you.
> Deep peace of Christ to you.

Saturday: restless for home

> You have made us for yourself, O Lord, and our heart is restless until it finds its rest in you.
>
> (St Augustine, *Confessions*)

> How lovely is your dwelling-place,
> O LORD of hosts!
> My soul longs, indeed it faints
> for the courts of the LORD;
> my heart and my flesh sing for joy
> to the living God.
> Even the sparrow finds a home,
> and the swallow a nest for herself,
> where she may lay her young,
> at your altars, O LORD of hosts,
> my King and my God.
>
> (Psalm 84.1–3)

> In my Father's house there are many dwelling-places. If it were not so, would I have told you that I go to prepare a place for you? (John 14.2)

In spring and autumn, many birds migrate. European swallows spend the winter in Africa, south of the Sahara, in Arabia and on the Indian subcontinent. British swallows fly between Britain and South Africa. They have two homes, two places to dwell, and a place here where they make their nests and provide for their young.

Swallows fly at 35mph, for 200 miles a day, and we are rightly amazed that they know when and where to go. They migrate in order to find food, and we can forget that it's a dangerous business. There's a high cost – many die of exhaustion and starvation as well as from storms along the way.

As swallows fly back and forth across the continents seeking food and a safe place for their young, so in the last few years have we seen human beings do the same in the biggest migrant or refugee crisis since the 1940s. For human beings, there is a clear goal: refuge, safety and food, a new place to dwell, somewhere to start a new life. The journey is dangerous, as we know from the news, and too many don't survive. As they seek protection and asylum in new lands, they can be given refuge, a new home.

When my mother was in her last months, cared for in a nursing home, she asked me, 'I suppose this is my last home before heaven, isn't it?' I found it such a poignant thing to hear. She wasn't in her own home, and she knew she had to make the nursing home her home, but not for long, for heaven would be her destination. Her words shook me because I realized there was only one direction, a direction she chose to describe as towards home, heaven.

Human beings long for home, a place to dwell and settle. We invite people to make themselves at home. We spend much of our lives searching for home or in homemaking, and that's because like swallows we have two homes. We can never quite settle here on earth because we long for heaven.

'In my Father's house there are many dwelling-places [or rooms],' Jesus says. These are places that Jesus prepares for each of us and then comes to take us there. There is somewhere where we can dwell, be at peace, accepted, safe enough to start a new life. We can call that heaven or eternal life and it can start in the here and now. It often starts when we realize the limitations of earth as a home, like the psalmist who longs to be a swallow nesting in the courts of God.

Christians have two homes and that might well account for the restlessness and dissatisfaction we can feel even when we have much to be thankful for in this life. It can also account for the way in which, as we grow closer to God, we are less interested in some of the things of this life, like success or possessions. We resonate with Jesus' words about storing up treasures in heaven, rather than on earth.

Swallows know where to go and when it's time to migrate. Refugees are compelled to travel, despite the dangers, to find a new home and a new life. The disciples were unsure about how they would get to where Jesus was, how they would find the way, and so he declared, 'I am the way, the truth and the life.' Jesus, the way, is a path that is just as dangerous as the route that a migrating swallow or refugee takes, and Jesus, the way, has only one direction, to home and to life.

You have two homes, and Jesus – who is the way, truth and life – leads us from our earthly home to our heavenly one where we dwell in peace with God, ourselves and others. The way heads in one direction, and it's a risky way because truth is demanding and life opens us up to new possibilities, relationships and surprising perspectives. We make the journey through the stages of human life, following Christ and so maturing as we age. The journey is also inward so that our inner life, heart or soul settle and trust in God more deeply and quietly. We find we can more easily look back with compassion on ourselves and others from a more secure space. We remember in such a way as to integrate our history with our experience of God's grace and feel at home.

- Where and when are you most at home, in your earthly home and in places that you count as spiritual homes?
- As spring emerges, it is time to seek a place to nest and prepare to bring into being signs of risen life. As a sign of investing in hope and in life that will emerge some months ahead, why not plant something this week? Planting bulbs or seeds is an investment for late spring or summer. You will need to do some nurturing. Having been brought out of the dark and cold into the light, a bulb will largely take care of itself, whereas seedlings will need more tending. As you do this, reflect on aspects of yourself that need care and tending.

FALLING: THE THIRD WEEK

> Even though I walk through the darkest valley,
> I fear no evil;
> for you are with me . . . (Psalm 23.4)

This is the first of the next three weeks where the theme is set by the experiences of Peter. Resilience grows in the face of adversity. It is like a muscle that grows stronger because it is used. Peter's adversity consists of facing danger, arrest and death and then the trauma of Jesus being executed while he failed in his attempts to help. We have all had experiences from which we can see no way out, experiences of falling, falling apart, breaking up or breaking down. We also pray for and seek to help personally or give to agencies and charities that specialize in supporting those who are at breaking point in some way. As we reflect on falling we take with us, from the twenty-third psalm, the presence of God in the darkest valleys of human life. We know that Peter comes through. As we reflect and pray with his story, may it help us to be open to the light of healing and grace in our lives so that we might grow stronger in compassion for ourselves and others.

Prayers for the week

For the morning

Christ, whose glory fills the skies,
Christ, the true and only Light,
Sun of righteousness, arise,
Triumph o'er the shade of night;
Day-spring from on high, be near;
Day-star, in my heart appear.

Dark and cheerless is the morn
Unaccompanied by Thee;
Joyless is the day's return,
Till Thy mercy's beams I see,
Till they inward light impart,
Glad my eyes, and warm my heart.

Visit then this soul of mine,
Pierce the gloom of sin and grief;
Fill me, radiancy divine,
Scatter all my unbelief;
More and more Thyself display,
Shining to the perfect day.
(Charles Wesley, 1707–88)

For the evening

As our evening prayer rises before you, O God,
so may your mercy come down upon us
to cleanse our hearts
and set us free to sing your praise
now and for ever.
(Opening prayer for Evening Prayer
from *Common Worship: Daily Prayer*)

For forgiveness

Almighty and everlasting God, who hatest nothing that thou hast made, and dost forgive the sins of all them that are penitent: Create and make in us new and contrite hearts, that we worthily lamenting our sins, and acknowledging our wretchedness, may obtain of thee, the God of all mercy, perfect remission and forgiveness; through Jesus Christ our Lord. Amen.

(The collect for Ash Wednesday and every day in Lent, The Book of Common Prayer)

The Welcoming Prayer Method

There are three movements of the prayer:

Feel and sink into
what you are experiencing this
moment in your body.

'WELCOME' what you are experiencing
this moment in your body as an opportunity
to consent to the Divine Indwelling.

Let go by saying
'I let go of my desire for security, affection,
control and embrace this moment as it is.'

Used with permission of Contemplative Outreach, <www.contemplativeoutreach.org>. For more information see <www.contemplativeoutreach.org/category/category/welcoming-prayer>.

Words from Scripture

The LORD is near to the broken-hearted,
and saves the crushed in spirit.

(Psalm 34.18)

The sacrifice acceptable to God is a broken spirit;
a broken and contrite heart, O God, you will not despise.

(Psalm 51.17)

A psalm to read

Psalm 51

Monday: broken

> Very truly, I tell you, unless a grain of wheat falls into the earth and dies, it remains just a single grain; but if it dies, it bears much fruit. Those who love their life lose it, and those who hate their life in this world will keep it for eternal life. (John 12.24–25)

As a mother of a small child I became aware that my daughter or I would have to break something in order for her to understand what 'broken' meant. I remember looking around for a plate or mug I didn't care much about and wondering if I could engineer it slipping out of our fingers. I could often hear myself saying, 'Be careful with that or you'll break it', and see her nodding, knowing that 'careful' was important and that 'broken' was a bad thing, to be avoided, but her puzzled look made me realize she had no comprehension of what broken was.

I longed for my daughter to understand what broken meant, to learn about brokenness with things that didn't matter much, so that I could help her avoid breaking things that did matter. I did know that I couldn't protect her from a broken heart or failure, but as parents do, I put a lot of energy into trying to protect my child from unnecessary pain.

Pain, struggle and suffering are an ordinary part of the human life-cycle. The spiritual writer and Franciscan priest Richard Rohr, in his book *Falling Upward: A spirituality for the two halves of life* (SPCK, 2012), suggests that there is a key time of suffering out of which we are transformed and change the direction of our lives. In the important process of building our life, establishing our identity, home and relationships, we journey through the first half of life. However, the journey to strive successfully is followed by a second journey, often in midlife, because some experience of falling down, brokenness or failure has us at a crisis point or crossroads. This time is the foundation for spiritual growth, a falling upwards where loss of control broadens our horizons and deepens our lives.

Jesus speaks of the need for a seed to be broken apart in order to grow and of how clinging to the trappings of our earthly life means we can lose the very heart of what life is about. Experiences of brokenness come in many forms. In some it is what others have done to us, in others a bereavement, disaster or illness, sometimes a situation of our own making. We used to use the term 'broken homes' of households after a marriage has ended. We tend not to use the term any more because the word 'broken' implies a judgement of a family. The brokenness of a relationship might be its dysfunctionality and the ending of the marriage the opportunity for healing and a new life. Even if brokenness does not imply that a life or relationship is beyond repair, or irredeemable, it does imply an ending of sorts.

The concept of falling evokes loss of control, an inability to keep all the balls in the air and so our lives falling apart. Human beings come through break-downs and break-ups. As Christians, we may well think of the doctrine of the Fall when Adam and Eve disobeyed God in the garden of Eden, blamed each other and were expelled. That was a fall from grace. Falling upwards is a fall into grace, a breaking open in which God is near.

Shame and guilt can drag us down. Many of us can feel guilty for things we are not guilty for and carry shame because of what has been done or said to us. There are also sins we know we need to bring before God for forgiveness, and repent and say sorry if that is possible. It is perfectly acceptable to offer our broken spirit to God. God will receive our brokenness and does not despise us. God has mercy on us because of his steadfast love. Whatever is sinful can be washed away.

My experience as a priest and pastor is that there are those who seek forgiveness, but whatever is troubling them is not something for which they need forgiveness, because they have not sinned. Accepting that we have been caught up in a situation, or sinned against, is hard to bear. When we can see we have been treated as an object rather than as a person, we see we were a victim at that time. Today we use the term 'survivor' rather than 'victim' to acknowledge that what was once the case is no longer, that we have come through, and our personhood is respected. This is a process that happens over time and when we take the opportunities to engage with our memories. It is healing that is needed, a reframing of the past to bring into the present a new perspective.

Living through a period of suffering can have us gritting our teeth and turning away from others because the vulnerability is hard to bear and we fear being pitied or judged. Holding fast to our intrinsic worth as human and being open to other human beings who will support us by their care, affirmation and presence is the path to a new quality of life.

We find Peter as a broken man, in the early dawn of Good Friday. But we know about Peter because his brokenness is not the end of the story.

- As you consider experiences of falling or brokenness in your own life, personal, professional, in those you know and in the world of which we are a part, can you call a person, relationship or event to mind and stay with the sadness of it, for a little time, to recognize the impact of it? Can you go deep enough to begin to feel that the story is not over yet, that something new can emerge, even if you have no idea what it might be?

Tuesday: losing control

> Then a servant-girl, seeing him in the firelight, stared at him and said, 'This man also was with him.' But he denied it, saying, 'Woman, I do not know him.' (Luke 22.56–57)

When there has not been some downfall we can point to in our lives, and if we are quite successful, we can imagine that we are in control of what happens to us. Sometimes I am aware that I am putting a great deal of energy into avoiding getting something wrong. I'm holding everything together by a fear of failure or of being disapproved of. This is a kind of perfectionism and it takes up a lot of energy. If I make a mistake, like getting a parking ticket or missing a train, I may fail to mention it because I feel foolish and defensive. Sometimes I have pretended that nothing is wrong or said something doesn't matter when it does. It's as if I have wanted to believe myself to be invincible. I don't want to admit that I am human, that I am not in control.

Peter found himself losing control on the night that Jesus was arrested. He began the night convinced of his ability to prevent things going wrong, to ensure success for Jesus' cause, even single-handedly if the others were to fail. The night went downhill for Peter, not just because of the dramatic events, but because of the small, easily understandable lapses.

We might all have fallen asleep after a heavy meal, not realizing that keeping watch and keeping close were that important. No doubt we have all played up or played down our association with someone in order to discover the lie of the land. We may have been non-committal so that we can discover someone's opinion about our friend or our boss, or in the face of someone's hostility pulled back from admitting our involvement with a group or organization. Those denials of Jesus by Peter can seem like that. They can seem like white lies to buy Peter time to find out what was happening to Jesus, or enabling him to escape from danger.

The crowing cockerel reminded Peter that Jesus had said he would deny him. Then there was the look Jesus gave him, having heard his friend say he didn't know him. The bitter tears are enough for us to realize the devastating impact of these. Peter wept as a broken man. He had let Jesus down, not been true to himself, and the relationship felt broken, damaged beyond repair. Peter's sense of himself, his self-image, was also shattered. He had declared to everyone that he would stand by Jesus and he failed.

Small actions and a few words may not be significant in terms of events. Peter denying he knew Jesus did not directly cause his execution, but it did add to his suffering. The impact was in their relationship, the brokenness of which was sealed by Jesus' death. We know the story, and so know that this was only for a few days. We don't know whether Peter, in the meantime, kept what had happened a secret, or whether he talked up his courage or his guilt to himself or the others. In so many things we are not directly responsible for the way things have turned out, but somehow we have helped things go in a particular direction by our behaviour and relationships have been compromised.

Periods of brokenness can be the means for deep spiritual change in our lives. Small failures such as breaking a vase, or forgetting an appointment, can also make us aware and be triggers for reflection, action and growth. We realize anew that we get tired, make mistakes or miss someone. We realize that a small word or action can have far-reaching consequences. The impact of something seemingly small can go deep within us, especially if it causes us to remember how we felt when something similar happened in the past. We feel past hurts in the present, and when we recognize that is what they are, we need not act out of them or be driven by them now. They are scars we are aware of, not open wounds. Acknowledging the past hurt to ourselves prevents us expressing it in one of those small ways whose impact causes harm we do not intend. Rather than avoiding or diminishing the impact of these feelings when we sense them, we can learn from what they have to teach us. Often this is best done by naming a feeling as it comes. It may be that we can't consider it until later.

The Welcoming Prayer was written by Father Thomas Keating, a Trappist monk and priest, born in 1923. He is known as one of the architects of Centering Prayer, a contemporary method of contemplative prayer. Such praying is particularly attentive to feelings and to the body. In the three movements of the prayer, the first requires you to feel and sink into what you are experiencing in your body. You then deliberately welcome whatever that feeling is as an opportunity to consent to whatever God will show you. In the third movement, you seek to let go by saying, 'I let go of my desire for security, affection, control and embrace this moment as it is.'

This is a prayer to pray when you experience or are aware of a painful or difficult feeling. Acknowledging what it is you are clinging to or fearful of and seeking to let it go enables you to then consider how you speak and act in the light of what you are aware of in yourself and having offered it to God.

Admitting our humanity, with its failures and pain, is a necessary part of the journey of maturity. We can rarely drive or control events, but if we do not play our part with integrity that also has an impact. Peter denied he knew Christ. His recognition of his fall and his response to Jesus' forgiveness was to become his path to healing and freedom.

- Is there a recent feeling that you can identify, allow it to sink in, welcome it and let it go? You may want to use the Welcoming Prayer.

Wednesday: the cockerel at daybreak

At that moment, while he was still speaking, the cock crowed. The Lord turned and looked at Peter. Then Peter remembered the word of the Lord, how he had said to him, 'Before the cock crows today, you will deny me three times.' And he went out and wept bitterly.

(Luke 22.60–62)

For it is the God who said, 'Let light shine out of darkness', who has shone in our hearts to give the light of the knowledge of the glory of God in the face of Jesus Christ. But we have this treasure in clay jars, so that it may be made clear that this extraordinary power belongs to God and does not come from us.

(2 Corinthians 4.6–7)

In August 1999, I witnessed the total solar eclipse when on I was on holiday in northern France. The moon passed between the earth and the sun, blocking direct sunlight and turning day into darkness. The eerie atmosphere was deepened by the silence of the natural world. Animals sensing that it was night became silent, dogs stopped barking, birds stopped singing, but as the moon passed over and the sun emerged the cockerel crowed. It was odd to have the call of daybreak after a night only a few minutes long, but I felt that the crowing signalled the end of an unnatural scary time and the return of familiar day.

A cockerel provides a wake-up call and heralds the return of daylight. When Peter heard the crowing, he was in the middle of denying that he knew Jesus. It was then that Jesus turned and looked at him. His first response was to weep. What would become of this broken man at daybreak?

The psychologist Martin Seligman (1909–84) wrote that when we hit rock bottom, our ability to recover can be stunted by what he calls the three Ps. These are Personalization, the belief that we are at fault; Pervasiveness, the belief that an event will affect all areas of our life; and Permanence, the belief that the aftershocks of the event will last for ever. When life has fallen apart in some way, you can sometimes hear a voice in your head saying that your whole life is dreadful, it is your fault that it's dreadful and it's always going to be like that.

We tend to focus on Peter denying Jesus because it is easy to put ourselves in his position and know we would do, even have done, something similar. But Peter is a resilient disciple from whom we can learn and not label as the one who denied Jesus. Peter, unlike Judas, comes through his experience of Jesus' death to experiencing his resurrection life by resisting the inner voices of the three Ps. Jesus wasn't crucified because Peter denied he knew him. Had Peter given in to the first P of Personalization he would have considered it all to have been his fault and overplayed his role. There are times when we feel bad about a situation and want to blame ourselves, perhaps preferring to wallow. Peter might have given in to believing that by denying Jesus he was thoroughly reprehensible, that his failure to stand by Jesus pervaded into all areas of his life. He would have given in to Pervasiveness. There are times when we quickly fear that everything in our lives has fallen apart when we have made a mistake. It can turn us in on ourselves and lead to a sense of Permanence that nothing now will change from this awful situation.

Victor Frankl in Auschwitz called to mind the face of his wife and found it stirred him, giving him strength by reminding him that he was loved and valuable. Jesus looked at Peter and Peter remembered. He remembered that Jesus, only a few hours previously, had predicted that he would deny him. But it wasn't the only thing he would remember. Peter would remember that Jesus had predicted he would suffer and die. He would remember the time when Jesus rescued him from the waves of Lake Galilee and asked him then why he had so little faith. Perhaps he remembered that at the Last Supper Jesus had also told him that he had prayed for him, that his faith would not fail, and then pointed to a future by saying, 'When once you have turned back, strengthen your brothers' (Luke 22.32). The memories involving those we love and who love us are very powerful. Reflecting on the situation we are in prevents us from spiralling down into self-blame and despair. Being able to remember that we are loved and valuable is life-giving in a dark place. Remembering how we have come through before and who has helped us is a strong thread in helping us come through again.

After a dark night, the cockerel didn't only remind Peter that Jesus knew him well enough to know what would happen; the crowing also heralded the light of a new day.

Leonard Cohen (1934–2016) in his song 'Anthem' famously writes that everything has a crack in it. That's how light can get in. When we feel life is breaking apart, not holding together, and we'll crack, we may find that the crack, like the crowing of a cockerel, signals that one period of darkness is over and it is time to notice the light. If we look at where the crack is, where the light is shining through, we can also expect more to emerge. Cohen writes that we must ring the bells that we can, and forget a perfectionism that keeps out the light.

St Paul described Christians as clay jars that contain the treasure of God's light. Clay jars are fragile, easily cracked and broken. Human beings, mortal creatures that we are, reveal the extraordinary light of God, which created and recreates us all. Christ knew that Peter, a human being, would crack under strain and he had prayed that Peter's faith wouldn't fail. His faith did not fail. When we break down, there is new room for light and faith that we are looked on by Christ, who knows our weakness and recreates us.

- Are you aware, in yourself or another, of a tendency when something goes wrong to slip down the road that leads to the problem becoming personalized, pervasive and permanent? Spend some time thinking through an example of this and reframing it.
- Might you offer support and encouragement to someone struggling in a dark period that could help that person to see where the light will come?

Thursday: the heart of God

Which one of you, having a hundred sheep and losing one of them, does not leave the ninety-nine in the wilderness and go after the one that is lost until he finds it? When he has found it, he lays it on his shoulders and rejoices. And when he comes home, he calls together his friends and neighbours, saying to them, 'Rejoice with me, for I have found my sheep that was lost.' (Luke 15.4–6)

I understand three ways of contemplating motherhood in God. The first is the foundation of our nature's creation; the second is his taking of our nature, where the motherhood of grace begins; the third is the motherhood at work.

The mother's service is nearest, readiest and surest: nearest because it is most natural, readiest because it is most loving, and surest because it is truest. No one ever might or could perform this office fully, except only him. We know that all our mothers bear us for pain and for death. O, what is that? But our true mother Jesus, he alone bears us for joy and for endless life, blessed may he be.

(Mother Julian of Norwich,
The Revelations of Divine Love,
chapters 59 and 60)

Mothers and grandmothers often say that the best presents they can receive are the home-made ones, especially those made by a child. It is showing love that is important, the personal investments and thoughtfulness, not the money spent. It is only natural to expect to see all those red hearts from Valentine's Day turn up on Mother's Day. It strikes me that there are three shapes we could focus on which reveal something of God's love for us and how love connects us to the world; they are the heart, the circle and the cross.

The shape of a heart conveys the warmth we feel in our hearts when we think of those we love. We are conscious of our hearts beating inside us, providing the means of life for our body. Our heart responds to our body, which is responding to the world. The electrical impulses work so that our heartbeat slows down when the body signals it is asleep, or speeds up when it signals we are in a panic. Our heart makes possible the fuel we need to respond and to act. Our life, first heard these days as a heartbeat during a scan in pregnancy, is given to us by God through our mothers, in what we describe as the miracle of birth. Hearts symbolize not just life but also love, because human life comes about because of relationships where we are nurtured. When we use the many heart emojis, if we do, we don't just indicate that we are alive; we use them to connect to someone else, to say that we are interested or love someone.

The shape of a circle is sometimes used to symbolize a hug. It contains, holds and embraces. I have noticed that what really counts, at certain times of year, for many of us, is the family gathering together. Mothers in particular seem to long for the circle of their love to be complete, for everyone to be together. I have noticed this when a mother is dying, and indeed it is true, not only for mothers, that a person will hang on when death is near, to be able to say farewell. Love and gathering together – these two shapes of a heart and a circle – capture something very important about human relationships, especially mothering, which reveals much about God's love for us.

Mother Julian of Norwich writes a great deal about Jesus as our mother and motherhood found in God. The heart of God yearns for everyone to be included in the circle of love. One of the best-known and loved parables is that of the lost sheep. The shepherd has 99 other animals in his flock, but it's not about how many you have. The point is that one is lost and must be found, rescued and brought back safely. So, the shepherd, just like the woman looking for a lost coin (Luke 15.8–10), searches until the flock or the necklace of coins is complete.

When Jesus dies on the cross, the writer of John's Gospel described him as drawing the whole world to himself (John 12.32). This sense of gathering all to God in love gets another shape – a cross as well as a heart and a circle. The heart of God responds and acts. Jesus our mother draws us into the circle of God's love, shown by the cross, and the Holy Spirit gives us what we need to respond and act in love to others.

Mothering Sunday, rather than Mother's Day, is a day of refreshment in the austere season that is Lent. John the Baptist, that figure who calls us to make a straight way for the Lord in the wilderness of Lent, tells us that he can baptize us with water, but Jesus will baptize us with the fire of the Holy Spirit. It is the love of our parents that brings us to baptism, and the power of the Holy Spirit that ignites our hearts to love God and brings us into the circle of the body of Christ. From there we grow up and, as we follow Christ, grow into an ability to live compassionately beyond our families and friends. We become able to bear the costs of love, shown in the cross, to reveal the liberating life of God as we work for justice and peace in God's world.

Motherhood comes with a realization that we are all connected to each other and need the help of the wider society to provide what a child needs. Becoming a parent motivates many people to work towards a better society for their children. Have you noticed that the presents we give on Mother's Day are also like the ones we see in church on Mothering Sunday? We give flowers, chocolates, even candles. They are gifts to be shared, in keeping with what we celebrate about motherhood today, whoever offers it. In mothering, love is shared, extended from one child to another who comes along, and wider, for love is not quantifiable; it does not run out, but deepens, extends and grows.

On Mothering Sunday, we are grateful for the life given to us. It was a gift that involved pain for our sake. In most cases it was accompanied by gifts of love and care because those who mother us share their lives and their love. Mothering doesn't always go well. Often, though, our mothers have given of themselves physically, emotionally and spiritually over many years in many ways. Though we have always been thankful for this, it is only as we have matured that we have appreciated the nature of the gift given to us. Today the best of mothering provides us with an insight into the heart of God, who draws us into the circle of his love. This comes about through the death of Jesus on the cross and the resurrection to a way of life where the fire of the Holy Spirit brings comfort, truth and peace.

God's mothering involves pain that brings life, and we are called to mother one another, be someone who brings life, bears pain, and draws others, again and again, into the circle of the heart of God.

- Thank God for all those who, as midwives of life and love, help to bring Christ to birth in you. How will you mark this mothering – by gift, word or your own mothering of another?

Friday: gone fishing

> Gathered there together were Simon Peter, Thomas called the Twin, Nathanael of Cana in Galilee, the sons of Zebedee, and two others of his disciples. Simon Peter said to them, 'I am going fishing.' They said to him, 'We will go with you.' They went out and got into the boat, but that night they caught nothing. (John 21.2–3)

In the UK in recent years there has been a national campaign to get people taking part in physical exercise, to get them off the couch and looking after their physical and mental health. The 5k and 10k 'parkruns' in communities across the country enable people to run together and meet the 'Couch to 5k' challenge. The spin-offs are the social and community benefits of people forming relationships with fellow participants and also raising money for charity.

Running gets you back in touch with yourself. The programme gets you running five kilometres in a few weeks, but it begins gradually. You feel your strength when you run. The rhythmic pounding of your feet takes you into your body and mind, mirroring your heartbeat and breath, making you conscious of your breathing. You become more aware of your feelings, especially those associated with frustration, motivation, satisfaction and patience. Running locates you in yourself, but when you run with others, strangers or friends, you become aware of the difference others make by their encouragement and by the nature of healthy competition.

When life is difficult we are forced back on ourselves and our resources. Retreating for a time can help us to take stock and work out the next move. Peter goes back to Galilee, somewhere familiar from which he can work out what has changed and what has been lost. He hasn't lost his ability to fish, or the boat presumably, and there's always a living to make, so he goes off fishing. Doing something that gives you a sense of control in life and being in touch with something familiar, especially if physical, is very valuable. We need time to be distracted from the confusion and pain of a situation to think and feel. Familiar, rhythmic physical activity can be just what we need, whether it is mowing the lawn, walking, swimming or fishing.

Peter retreated to Galilee after the crucifixion. He returned to the place that was home and where he had once had a role as a fisherman. He returned to familiar activity and to the place where he had first met Jesus. From this perspective, he could see what was different in him and for him. Going fishing was what he had decided he needed to do, but he was happy for the others to come too.

When we know someone is having a difficult time we can wonder whether to leave the person alone or not. We can be tempted to think we should provide some company. Of course, we should ask the person what he or she wants, but be aware that both are important. Solitude is necessary for the internal processing of our thoughts and feelings. When we think of solitude we often think of solitary confinement, but in that case it is the confinement, the sensory deprivation and inability to move much that is the punishment. Being alone, especially somewhere beautiful, is very healing.

To have others care for us by inviting us to a meal, allowing us to ring or drop in, listening to how we are, is also vital. Friends who accept us, no matter what, are what we need, and also to turn away from those who are inclined to blame or intrude with many questions. Often it may be just a few trusted people that we confide in, but we are grateful for the wider kindness and can reassure others with the comment, 'Thank you for asking.' There is an important halfway house between being alone and with others. Activities where we are with others, like a concert or a run, can provide us with the opportunity to reflect but in a way that is time-bound, uninterrupted and accompanied. After bereavement, in particular, it can be hard to gauge how much you will need to be out with others and how much time to take just to be by yourself. The emptiness is present in both, just as Peter found: though he fished, he caught nothing.

If we imagine a wooden notice saying 'Gone Fishing', we know it means someone has jacked in whatever he or she was doing, for the afternoon, perhaps for longer, but will return having had the space required to carry on. This Sunday, Mothering Sunday or Refreshment Sunday, marks the halfway point of Lent and provides a day for rest and revival. Traditionally you lay aside the discipline of Lent, to be refreshed, before taking it up again. In the past, domestic servants could go home to their mothers. We can have a glass of wine or eat chocolate.

Peter returned to his home in Galilee. As Mothering Sunday approaches, many of us will return to or remember familiar places and activities associated with our mothers and our upbringing. This may bring great joy and gratitude. It may bring tender and mixed memories and emotions. In every life and every family there are times of difficulty because of circumstances, death and difficult relationships. We have to consider, as adults, the patterns and boundaries we will set with our family of origin. Retreating can be necessary and helpful when things are exploitative or difficult. Wisdom is needed to decide how long this should be for, or what factors need to be in place for change. Where things are complicated, careful contact, perhaps by post, can provide a steady and peaceful way to relate.

Our mothers brought us to birth and so are the primary illustration for Mothering Sunday, which celebrates Mother Church, the community of Christians who by God's grace help to bring Christ to birth in us. The family of the Church, of course, has the same kinds of disagreements and difficulties as human families. What can be different is the way in which, accompanied by the grace of God, we approach them.

- Will you break from your Lenten discipline on Sunday? If you have already lapsed, what have you learned about yourself, your motivation and endurance?
- In the second half of Lent, that is, for the next three weeks, will you set a different discipline for your well-being, body and soul?

Saturday: wise as serpents, gentle as doves

> See, I am sending you out like sheep into the midst of wolves; so be wise as serpents and innocent as doves. (Matthew 10.16)

Throughout my life I have been able to call to mind, all too easily, the psychedelic eyes of Kaa, the snake from *The Jungle Book* by Rudyard Kipling, originally published in 1894, though known more popularly in the 1967 or 2016 Disney films. It is from the film that I see Kaa and hear the singing for Mowgli, the man cub, to trust in him. I've been haunted by the hypnotic swirling and hissing with which he tries to capture the boy and eat him. I've also been fascinated by the way in which Mowgli is able to come to his senses, to who he is, in that moment and so manages to resist the hypnosis. Kipling portrayed Kaa as trustworthy, a confidant to the man cub, Mowgli. Kaa was an old long yellowish Indian rock python in the original tale, who saved Mowgli's life on multiple occasions. In the films, however, Kaa, who is male in 1967 and female in 2016, is untrustworthy, preying on the child and playing into the cultural view of snakes as devious.

So when we hear Jesus recommending that, in the face of the dangers of our lives as Christians, we should be like a serpent or snake, we are a bit bemused. In fact, we need the wisdom Jesus attributes to the snake in order to discern what he might mean. Animals are morally neutral but they symbolize qualities for us. Jesus says he sends us out like sheep among wolves. Now, Mowgli the man cub was protected and brought up by a wolf, so not all wolves have proved dangerous, but it is reasonable to expect a sheep to be eaten alive by a pack of wolves. Snakes in the Judeo-Christian tradition are associated with evil, so their wisdom is described as being crafty, sneaky, used to manipulate and trap prey.

We are Christ's flock, sheep who can experience the world as hostile, personally and because we live out our lives as Christian disciples. We need to be resilient in the face of danger, recover and grow stronger. Difficulty and danger can have us acting like a snake. We might lash out, bite people's heads off, try to set traps, manipulate or seek to isolate people. These are not the qualities of the snake we should cultivate in order to face the uncertainties and difficulties of life, though hardship can breed them and we are wise to guard against them, especially in difficulty. The snake's wisdom resides in being alert and patient, in a timeliness and shrewdness that acts and is effective. When life is difficult, it helps to be alert to the time when change for the better is possible, in a relationship or in a particular situation, and when it is not. Acting shrewdly and speaking at the right time can bring relief and protection. The snake also sheds its skin so that it can grow. It has to leave behind what it no longer needs in order to mature, just as we do.

The wisdom of the snake is balanced in Jesus' phrase by the innocence or gentleness of the dove. Doves were ritually clean animals that could be offered as innocent victims in sacrifice for sin in the Temple, in the time of Jesus. To be as innocent as a dove calls to mind the Hippocratic Oath revered by the medical profession where the first consideration is one of abstaining from harm: 'do no harm'. Whatever you say and do, make sure you are not going to do more harm than good. Sometimes not saying and holding back is what constitutes the innocence we should strive for.

Doves can also teach us something about being in touch with our deepest nature, by their settling and homing. Some doves live in dovecotes, and 'homing' is the word used to settle the doves into the dovecotes that have sections for each pair. Some doves, which are part of the same family as pigeons, have a homing instinct, in that they can be relied upon to return home, wherever they have been taken to. To be as gentle as a dove invites us to remember where home is and to return to God however many times we are sent out. Then there are the turtle doves, which are symbols of friendship and love because they are known for their affection to their mate and their soft purring call. To be as gentle as a dove, the symbol of peace, involves being at peace, in the presence of God, which is home. It means having the courage to return there from the places of danger and failure that you have been in, in order to build peace in Christ's name.

The pain of things going wrong can be soothed as we settle again in the presence of God. To make peace in the world, our peace needs to come from within. When we settle and are at home within and with God, as a dove might be, we will be more able to greet others with the olive branches of compassion and hospitality. With patient waiting and alertness we can be wise like a snake and act at the right time to bring about peace. Mowgli resists being hypnotized by Kaa, the snake, because he comes to his senses just in time. Like a dove, our peace is within, deep and settled, offered to others gently. In the presence of wolves that would devour peace, we must act like a snake with timeliness and wisdom, do no harm and forge peace effectively in our world.

- When danger is near, are you conscious of the triggers that, if you are alert to them, help you to come to your senses and seek the safety of returning home and to peace?

FAITHFUL: THE FOURTH WEEK

> You are with me;
> your rod and your staff –
> they comfort me.
> (Psalm 23.4)

In this week, and next, we go beyond Lent in the life of Peter in order to reflect on the way in which he and we, as disciples, grow in resilience and maturity. When we hit rock bottom, when things in our lives or in someone else's life fall apart, there is much that can be done to set a framework for coping and recovery. There are externals to change, which might be our diet, for example, and also inner patterns of thought to adjust. There is something deep within us too, the God at the ground of our being, who provides the catalyst to bring everything together, our hearts and minds, in such a way as to enable us to take a step forward into a more hopeful future. We can meet God in the desert experiences, those that simply come upon us, unexpectedly and unwelcome, and also in the physical and mental disciplines we set in order to deepen our faith and trust in God to guide us into the future.

I have titled this week Faithful because in the adversity of our lives God's faithfulness draws us through what is dark and difficult and we find comfort – a word that speaks of being fortified and strengthened. In this week we see Jesus meeting Peter again, in the second experience that comes as a group of three in Peter's life. Jesus is able to bring about a reconciliation and restoration of Peter by his ability to convey his forgiveness. I invite you to think about what has brought you through difficult times and relationships. It may be that you will focus on a particular experience in the present or in the past and discover, by the grace of God, some of the gifts in the experience that it is time to acknowledge or use. You might focus on becoming more Christ-like in your ability to bring about the healing of relationships. God's presence and faithfulness are comforting due to the use of the tools of a shepherd, the rod and the staff. The rod is used to defend the sheep, to prod and prompt. The staff is a symbol of authority and the shepherd uses the hooked end to get hold of lambs in danger, as well as straying sheep, and bring them close, back to the fold.

As we mature as disciples we can look back on difficult times and see the golden threads of God's faithfulness in events and people. We realize what we could not have seen before, that God is sovereign. Many of us are surprised to find that we would not change things, because of the precious nature of the treasure we gained. We recognize too that we are more accepting of others, more empathetic, less needing to compare and judge, more able to follow Christ in the context of our own story. As we grow in resilience and maturity we recognize that there will be adversity to come in our lives and know we will be able to find the resources and supports to meet those challenges when they arrive.

Prayers for the week

For the morning

O God, the author of peace
and lover of concord,
to know you is eternal life,
to serve you is perfect freedom.
Defend us your servants
from all assault of our enemies;
that we, surely trusting in your defence,
may not fear the power of any adversaries;
through Jesus Christ our Lord.
(A morning prayer from
Common Worship: Daily Prayer)

For the evening

Visit this place, O Lord, we pray,
and drive far from it the snares of the enemy;
may your holy angels dwell with us and guard us in peace,
and may your blessing be always upon us;
through Jesus Christ our Lord.
(Traditional night prayer)

The choristers' prayer

Bless, O Lord, us Thy servants who minister in Thy temple.
Grant that what we sing with our lips we may believe in our hearts,
and what we believe in our hearts we may show forth in our lives.
Through Jesus Christ our Lord. Amen.

Hymn

Great is Thy faithfulness, O God my Father;
There is no shadow of turning with Thee,
Thou changest not, Thy compassions they fail not,
As Thou hast been, Thou forever wilt be.

Great is Thy faithfulness!
Great is Thy faithfulness!
Morning by morning new mercies I see.
All I have needed Thy hand hath provided,
Great is Thy faithfulness, Lord, unto me!

Summer and winter and springtime and harvest,
Sun, moon, and stars in their courses above,
Join with all nature in manifold witness
To Thy great faithfulness, mercy and love.

Pardon for sin and a peace that endureth,
Thine own dear presence to cheer and to guide;
Strength for today, and bright hope for tomorrow,
Blessings all mine, with ten thousand beside.
(Thomas Chisholm, 1866–1960)

Words from Scripture

Sing to the LORD a new song,
for he has done marvellous things.
(Psalm 96.1)

You have delivered my soul from death,
and my feet from falling,
so that I may walk before God in the light of life.
(Psalm 56.13)

A psalm to read

Psalm 63

Monday: holding and healing

> He said to him the third time, 'Simon son of John, do you love me?' Peter felt hurt because he said to him the third time, 'Do you love me?' And he said to him, 'Lord, you know everything; you know that I love you.' Jesus said to him, 'Feed my sheep.' (John 21.17)

> Jacob was left alone; and a man wrestled with him until daybreak. When the man saw that he did not prevail against Jacob, he struck him on the hip socket; and Jacob's hip was put out of joint as he wrestled with him. Then he said, 'Let me go, for the day is breaking.' But Jacob said, 'I will not let you go, unless you bless me.' So he said to him, 'What is your name?' And he said, 'Jacob.' Then the man said, 'You shall no longer be called Jacob, but Israel, for you have striven with God and with humans, and have prevailed.' Then Jacob asked him, 'Please tell me your name.' But he said, 'Why is it that you ask my name?' And there he blessed him. (Genesis 32.24–29)

If you have ever been to the Tate Britain or seen a picture of *Jacob and the Angel* by Sir Jacob Epstein, you will remember a huge sculpture, greater than life-size, of Jacob and another figure with wings, upright and facing each other. They are locked together and could be holding each other in a tender embrace or one could have the other in a vice-like grip. The struggle between them ends in Jacob gaining the blessing he desires, but also being left with a disability that marks him out and is a constant reminder of that night of wrestling.

Jesus, like the angel who wrestles with Jacob, holds Peter through their first conversation after the crucifixion and resurrection in such a way that he is blessed. We cannot tell whether the conversation is full of half-smiles and warmth or has awkward pauses and a sense of the relationship on a precipice. Is there a struggle between them as they seek a way forward, or does it flow like a dance? Jesus mirrors Peter's three denials by asking three times, 'Do you love me more than these?' We don't know whether the question asks Peter if he loves Jesus more than the other disciples love him, more than he loves the other disciples or more than fishing. Jesus does not humiliate Peter. He crafts what he says in such a way that

Peter apologizes in his threefold response, by telling Jesus he knows everything. Though not explicit, there is a sense that Peter has shown he understands exactly what Jesus has forgiven him of and that it is good between them.

Jesus holds this conversation with the kind of firmness and gentleness you need to use to hold together two pieces of broken crockery you have just glued. Each side needs to placed back together carefully to fit. Too much pressure will erode or break one side further; not enough and they will not stay together. This encounter, like that of Jacob with the angel, reveals that meeting God does not make us passive but calls from within us a desire for life, blessing and love. In the face of creative and resurrection life we experience a surge towards grasping what could be. The struggle might be physical or it might be felt in the invisible and unconscious forces within us. We won't always be able to name them, as Jacob couldn't, but engaging with them will enable a breakthrough to a different kind of understanding and life.

Jesus' ability to bring about reconciliation doesn't leave Peter and Jesus in the place where they left off. It is a transformative experience for Peter to fall and then to find that Jesus' response is to be faithful to Peter. He had prayed that Peter's faith would not fail, that he would remember to return to the disciples just as much as he would remember Jesus had known he'd be faithless when the cock crowed.

Most of us can recall difficult conversations when we have struggled to say we have been hurt, or to listen to the impact of our behaviour on another, and struggled to be gentle enough so that the cracks and fragments of a relationship can be mended and put together again. Often it is the struggle in ourselves that has already gone on which enables us to seek blessing. We will have to have smoothed abrasive surfaces and applied a glue that is neither tacky nor too slippery.

Jesus doesn't just indicate that there are no hard feelings. He restores Peter to his position of being a disciple and tells him to feed his sheep, to tend his lambs. The healings that Jesus performed always had those healed restored to relationship. The point of reconciliation and healing is for there to be transformed lives. For Jacob it resulted in reconciliation with the twin brother he had wronged. For Peter it was to mean a tried and tested leading of the disciples in which he would exhibit greater wisdom and compassion.

Jesus holds Peter with a gentle firmness that brings, out of their broken relationship, healing. The disciples had been held together by their common purpose of following the Messiah, someone they had thought would lead a political uprising. The reasons they had come together couldn't be the reasons they stayed together. This is true in many relationships. You discover that the reasons you go to church, value your husband or keep in touch with someone have shifted. What holds you together is often deeper, perhaps less strained.

When life is particularly stressful we can feel that it is only pressure that is holding us together and if we stopped everything would fall apart. You may be aware of habits, such as defence mechanisms you employ, that once served you well, but you no longer need. Now might be an opportunity to relax them or let go of them completely. There may be an internally driven pressure, a fear of failure for example, that is causing you to be driven in a certain way of living. There are clearly external pressures too and some that perhaps you could let go of.

Lent is a time to consider our lives and relationships and what holds them together. What shifts would enable us to be open to healing or living in a more relaxed way? This might initially involve a struggle for blessing. We could be helped in this by trusting a skilled person to let us work through something or preparing ourselves to have a conversation that will be a risk but full of possibility for new perspective.

- Are there experiences of struggle that mark you out and leave you with reminders of what has been? Can you name what has shaped you since those marks and what shapes you now?
- Consider recent apologies you have offered and received. What about them liberated or restricted the relating, and what have you learned?
- Name some reasons why you began a project or relationship. What are the reasons now that mean you continue?

Tuesday: kintsugi – *the art of repairing with gold*

Jesus said to him, 'Feed my sheep'. (John 21.17)

Father-like He tends and spares us;
Well our feeble frame He knows.
In His hands He gently bears us,
Rescues us from all our foes.
Alleluia! Alleluia!
Widely yet His mercy flows.
(Henry F. Lyte, 1793–1847)

For five hundred years, *kintsugi*, 'joining with gold', has been practised in Japan as the art of mending. The story is of a fifteenth-century military commander, Ashikaga Yoshimasa, who was disappointed with the repair of his favourite, but broken, Chinese tea bowls. He asked the craftsmen to come up with some better method of repairing them and so a seam of lacquer and precious metal was used to restore them. These bowls are fragile and made of rigid pottery that cracks and breaks. The mending with lacquer mixed with powdered gold usually results in something more beautiful than the original. The philosophy behind this art of broken pieces is that nothing is ever truly broken. Using gold is an extravagance, you could argue, because it is cheaper to replace a piece of broken pottery than to mend it. The break, however, is an important part of the object's history and becomes more precious than it was before. Such an approach is connected to the Japanese idea of *wabi-sabi* which, in contrast to the Western values of perfection and symmetry, finds beauty in the damaged and imperfect. More than upcycling or preloved, the art of kintsugi draws attention to the life of a pot, once broken, repaired and continuing its life more beautiful than before the break.

The experience of suffering changes us. We cannot stay the same. We may know some people who even quite some time after a divorce, for example, are still as angry as ever and seem content to remain so. For many people the experience of being broken, though not pleasurable, has given a depth to their lives that means they don't wish an illness, for example, hadn't happened. The art of kintsugi is a reminder that the healing that comes from brokenness of any sort is precious. It draws attention to where the breaks are, where there is fragility, but they are honoured with gold. The experiences we don't wish on anyone become the very things that mark us out as distinctive and interesting. Each broken vessel is made unique and beautiful as the pieces are put back together, but unless you looked carefully or already knew, you would just see the golden pattern. People who have suffered and come through are often recognizable by an almost palpable presence. They are able, when you are low or hurting, to somehow impart some peace and hope that gives you what you need to take another step forward. You won't know the details of their story, but you experience the gold that comes from their healing. You might call these people holy, saints or wounded healers.

Our wounds make us who we are, but healed, we are used again. William Morris said that you should '*have nothing* in your house that you do not know to be useful, or believe to be *beautiful*'. Kintsugi restores objects to functionality and makes them beautiful. Being healed involves being ready to be used again. Discerning the time when you were ready can come in retrospect or you can be aware of it emerging and looking out for it. Usually it follows an inner shift where the way in which you approach your life is different alongside any external changes that occur.

Peter, restored by Jesus, is recalled to follow and given a new role, to feed Christ's sheep and tend his lambs. As a fisherman Peter had been called by Jesus to use his skills to catch people. As someone who had fallen and suffered, Jesus could now place Peter in the pastoral role of shepherd and teacher.

The experience of adversity often enables us to be more tolerant of our own and other people's imperfections. It makes us better able to support, mentor and care for others who are younger, inexperienced or vulnerable. It is true that helping others plays a role in our own healing. In giving back in some way, in recognition perhaps that we have had life returned, we find satisfaction, and also an inner healing. It is important to discern the right time to offer our experience to those in difficulty and also to look after ourselves. A healthy relationship that is forged between someone who has come through suffering and someone who is experiencing it brings about healing for both people. We call this a 'wounded healer' relationship. Wounded healers need to be aware that the wounds can still hurt and to take care of themselves in caring for others. Supervisors for those in intensive pastoral occupations as well as spiritual directors can be very helpful here when caring gets close to home. Sometimes caring can become too much for someone and he or she slips into being distant and at worst becomes abusive, an unhealed wounder, rather than a wounded healer.

The time when we sense that we are ready to be used again brings great joy. Henry F. Lyte, the writer of the hymn 'Praise, my soul, the King of heaven', describes the singer as standing before God, 'ransomed, healed, restored, forgiven, evermore His praise to sing'. We might describe a new more hopeful phase of life in different ways. Resilient people are identified by psychologists as those who live well and love well. Remade with the gold of grace, wisdom and compassion, they go on to live out these qualities as they offer themselves to others.

- How might you describe any inner shift that has led you to approach an aspect of your life differently? Have any come from a pain that you now value as gold?
- Is it time for you to recognize that you are ready, or nearly ready, to be used again?

Wednesday: my story

> 'Very truly, I tell you, when you were younger, you used to fasten your own belt and to go wherever you wished. But when you grow old, you will stretch out your hands, and someone else will fasten a belt around you and take you where you do not wish to go.' ([Jesus] said this to indicate the kind of death by which [Peter] would glorify God.) After this he said to him, 'Follow me.'
>
> Peter turned and saw the disciple whom Jesus loved following them; he was the one who had reclined next to Jesus at the supper and had said, 'Lord, who is it that is going to betray you?' When Peter saw him, he said to Jesus, 'Lord, what about him?' Jesus said to him, 'If it is my will that he remain until I come, what is that to you? Follow me!'
>
> (John 21.18–22)

In one of C. S. Lewis's chronicles of Narnia, *The Horse and His Boy* (HarperCollins, 2009), two children and two horses escape from misery and end up travelling together. Shasta, who has escaped being sold as a slave by a poor fisherman who wasn't his father, discovers by the end that he is a long-lost prince. Aravis, a high-born Tarkeener, had drugged her slave girl in order to escape, without a thought to the punishment the girl would get. Aravis gets wounded by the lion Aslan with the same number of scratches as the lashes inflicted on the girl, though, and through it learns empathy and compassion. The discipleship theme of the book is that we have to live our own story, respond with grace to the invitations life constantly provides, but not concern ourselves with the story another is called to live out. On the journey the horses and the children find their true identity and their 'bestest' selves, made possible by their ability to lay aside their assumptions and accept themselves and each other. They find home – for some it is a return, for others it is for the first time.

A few years ago, on the way through France, I ensured that we found ourselves at Chartres Cathedral on a Friday morning. During the summer months, the labyrinth is uncovered there for people to walk. The labyrinth is circular, just under 13 metres across, and set in the floor. The path leads you to the centre, which you can see, and out again, and you walk quietly, with others, following an outer journey that provides insight into your inner journey, the story of your life. A labyrinth takes you to its centre by twists and turns. It isn't a maze that blocks your path and tricks you, designed as a pastime. The labyrinth is designed to take you deeper into your life, to be walked as a prayer.

As I walked barefoot on the stone path I could see people ahead and people behind. At various places, I had to wait for others before I could continue. I walked alongside some people, often when we were on parallel paths and in the opposite direction to others. We were all on the same journey, had started from the same place, but some would finish at the centre and some would choose to take the path back to the edge. After a while, walking, I learned not to bump into the person ahead, or be frustrated because I was sure I was ahead of some person who now seemed ahead of me. Sometimes I felt closer to the centre than I was, and then all of a sudden, having felt on the edge, I got closer and then arrived.

I found walking the labyrinth an important lesson in learning to be non-judgemental and to follow the path I was on, regardless of where anyone else was. The labyrinth draws you in, to be in touch with yourself more deeply, and you travel towards the centre, your own centre. It is my story of following Christ that I should journey on, to its very centre, without worrying that I have taken too long or being smug that I am ahead.

Peter had just been told by Jesus that there was more suffering ahead for him. Once, he had resisted strongly the idea that there would be suffering for Jesus to fulfil his call. Here Peter seems to accept whatever the call is that Jesus makes on his life, but he wants to know about how others will fare. We have the sense that Jesus expects Peter, as he ages, to continue to grow and that losing control, as before, would play a part in it. Whether leading, being respected and in control, or weak and vulnerable, the call to follow Jesus is the same. There are patterns in Peter's life, of things happening three times and also of losing control. There are always opportunities to use what we have learned before, give back something we were given, make up in some way for where we fell down. These cycles and invitations to healing make us whole when we can respond to them. To do so will mean accepting ourselves, our situation and our call.

It's still natural to want to know, as Peter did, about other people.

Accepting ourselves, where we are and what God calls us to be and do, is a sign of maturity. It goes with not knowing the details of where we will be led, but trusting in God. It is wise not to compete and compare ourselves with others, but rather to accept them and where they are, neither judging them nor ourselves. They may be less grown up than we would like or more mature than we expected, but either way, in being called to follow Christ we are called to love them. We do not know the future. Peter knew it would involve suffering. Seasoned now by suffering and aware that, with Jesus, death and darkness is never the end of the story, he continued to follow. As we mature, our capacity to bear and overcome difficulty increases. Resilience can only grow in response to adversity. The direction and expression of resilience, as of following Christ, is compassion for ourselves and serving others.

- How might you deepen your own acceptance of your own life story?
- Are there invitations you seek, to right wrongs or give back, that will free you?
- What old or young person might you encourage this week in the journey of his or her life?

Thursday: untangling and binding

> Truly I tell you, whatever you bind on earth will be bound in heaven, and whatever you loose on earth will be loosed in heaven. Again, truly I tell you, if two of you agree on earth about anything you ask, it will be done for you by my Father in heaven. For where two or three are gathered in my name, I am there among them.'
>
> Then Peter came and said to him, 'Lord, if another member of the church sins against me, how often should I forgive? As many as seven times?' Jesus said to him, 'Not seven times, but, I tell you, seventy-seven times'.
>
> (Matthew 18.18–22)

I'm quite good at undoing knots and untangling balls of wool and string. In our house when someone can't undo the twisted silver chain of a necklace it is brought to me and I go and sit down somewhere peaceful and work on it. I'm not generally noted for being particularly patient and calm, but, for tangled threads, I know that these are the qualities I can summon up while someone else has got too frustrated with it. When it comes to untangling, calmness and patience are the only qualities that will work; pulling angrily will only make the knot tighter and probably break the threads.

Much sin occurs within our relationships because they get tangled in the normal course of things. We sin against each other in small and sometimes in much larger ways, through negligence, weakness and our own deliberate fault. Forgiveness, as a way of life, involves working away at loosening the knots that would prevent us finding a way through the complexities of relationships so that the fabric of our lives can be restored.

Forgiveness is a way of life for a Christian, but it isn't a call to be a doormat. Is that what Peter wondered when he asked Jesus how many times he should forgive? How many times is it reasonable to put up with someone before you are ground down, exploited, or you snap? Jesus tells Peter not to forgive seven times, but seventy-seven. He might have said: stop counting and start living in a way that shows you are free, secure and able, by God's grace, to let go and be open to love.

Forgiving does not mean letting someone off, accepting outrage or compromising justice. Sin has to be addressed and crimes reported. Sin is destructive and erodes both the sinner and the one sinned against. We all sin and are sinned against. Pretending that this isn't the case builds up within us, makes us tense so that we can feel it in our bodies, the tightness around our shoulders, knots in our muscles. Forgiveness is releasing others and being released from the sin that binds us.

Forgiving is a way of life, rather than keeping a score, and it is a lifelong process. God continues to be faithful to his people despite the faithlessness of his people that we read of through the pages of the Scriptures. Jesus is faithful to his love of Peter and shows us that for a Christian sin and death is never the end of the story. We are called to be faithful in following Christ on the way of forgiveness. We won't necessarily feel we are very far down the road. The important thing is that we are set in the right direction and taking what steps we can. It is only possible to forgive, ourselves and other people, through the grace of God and with the help of others. It is where two or three are gathered together, praying for God's intervention, that they can sense Jesus among them, and the opportunities for forgiveness and peace.

Jesus had told Peter that 'whatever you bind on earth will be bound in heaven, and whatever you loose on earth will be loosed in heaven.' Picture that tangled ball of wool and what you would need to do in order to untangle the threads to knit something. You have to find an end, follow the thread as far as you can and untangle by seeking a way through, loosening knots. You must make sure you wind it again evenly, or you'll just start another tangled ball.

When we try to force someone to see things our way, or refuse to listen, we tighten and tangle our lives and find we are bound by and to the negative thoughts and comments, the sins we have suffered and inflicted. We can't escape, but go over and over things and cannot find a loose end that could be the beginning of freeing up our lives.

Sin binds us to it and when we focus on that sin it can bind us more tightly. When you find it hard to forgive, focus on the freedom and release that forgiveness is, on the healing that can be brought about by God for you or another, with or without any other person involved. That will provide a way through, an opening, or space in you, in which you will find God can work.

St Patrick sought to bind himself to the strong name of the Trinity. The prayer we know as St Patrick's Breastplate was rewritten to be set to music in 1889 by the Irish poet Cecil Frances Alexander. She has secured it as a well-loved hymn. St Patrick prays to be bound, not to sin, but to God, the Trinity:

> I bind unto myself the name,
> The strong name of the Trinity,
> By invocation of the same,
> The Three in One and One in Three.

It's a prayer many say every day or in times of struggle. When we feel pulled towards resentment or self-blame we can call to mind the words that describe us as enveloped by Christ, secure and held:

> Christ be with me, Christ within me,
> Christ behind me, Christ before me,
> Christ beside me, Christ to win me,
> Christ to comfort and restore me.
> Christ beneath me, Christ above me,
> Christ in quiet, Christ in danger,
> Christ in hearts of all that love me,
> Christ in mouth of friend and stranger.

Forgiving others and ourselves frees us to live fully. We all have work to do to loosen or untangle threads that have tightened into knots in our lives. Perhaps once we or others pulled impatiently and the thread is fragile there. When you reuse wool, you take care at those points, but find that something new, strong and useful can be made. You might even knit a breastplate like St Patrick's to bind you to God who will protect you.

- Might you notice a loose thread in your life and begin to pray, following where it leads, and with care untangling so that you can see where God is and where God is leading you?

Friday: the buried treasure of our needs

> This is the greatest and first commandment. And a second is like it: 'You shall love your neighbour as yourself.' On these two commandments hang all the law and the prophets. (Matthew 22.38–40)

> Do not store up for yourselves treasures on earth, where moth and rust consume and where thieves break in and steal; but store up for yourselves treasures in heaven, where neither moth nor rust consumes and where thieves do not break in and steal. For where your treasure is, there your heart will be also. (Matthew 6.19–21)

Compassion fatigue is something we can identify in ourselves when we have become immune to and emotionally blunted by the trauma and bad news we see and hear about. We stop feeling the sadness and shield ourselves. We can zone out of conversations with our nearest and dearest while doing something else and are often seduced by the lure of a screen. Mobile phones distract us and we find ourselves doing something else in mid-conversation even when we didn't want to. We know the consequences of not paying attention to what other people are saying to us. We need too to pay attention to our needs, offer ourselves empathy and compassion. In doing so we discover a treasure within which enables our love and compassion to expand.

A counsellor, trained in active listening, will follow the foundational values of counselling set out by Carl Rogers (1902–87), the values of unconditional positive regard. He or she will seek to listen to us, be fully present to us. It is when we experience someone being fully present to us that we are touched deeply, able to open up. Such empathy is transforming, and to grow in compassion we each have to extend such empathy to ourselves. When we listen to someone else we can find our own anxiety or anger rising over something the other person has said. Taking time to be in touch with it, in another space, enables us to reflect on what it is about and not let it get in the way of our listening to someone else. In giving ourselves time and attention, especially when we feel hassled, vulnerable or frustrated, we give ourselves the chance to know what our needs really are and meet them.

Marshall Rosenberg (1934–2015), founder of NVC (Non-Violent Communication), developed a method of self-empathy in which you pay attention to those seemingly uncontrollable slips of the tongue, to lightning rage and to irritability. They are opportunities to become aware of the forces within you, not so much to understand them as to connect with the feelings and needs underneath them. When you have surprised yourself with the strength of feeling you're experiencing, you ask yourself: what is the longing of my heart? The answer is to be sought not in your mind, but in your body. Your body has grown tense, heavy and constricted, but when you can name and connect with the need, you feel a shift, a sigh perhaps, a relaxing of your body that is life-giving. Imagining what it would be like for the situation to be good, and how it would feel, is a helpful way of connecting with your unmet needs. Your unmet needs are the buried treasure, the qualities that when you connect with them give life.

This approach has to be done in a particular situation. On the morning we were going on holiday several years ago, I couldn't find one half of a toothbrush case I'd bought for each of us to use to stop the toiletry bag getting wet. I shouted at my whole family, accusing each person of stealing it. Clearly this was memorable, because jokes seem to abound still about why anyone would want to steal half of a toothbrush case. I have even received a pack of toothbrush cases as a birthday present. Now I can laugh with my family, but I couldn't for some time, until I had connected with the feelings and unmet needs that had derailed me then. Was I frustrated that morning because people had dumped their toiletries all over the floor and I needed order? Did I need some of them to follow through when they had said they would do their own packing and take responsibility for themselves? Was I anxious about us leaving on time and was it support that I needed, verbal or behavioural, to make it happen? Did I need thanks and appreciation for having sorted out so much in advance, including thinking of the toothbrush holders? At the time and when laughed at later, I was very conscious that no one thought that toothbrush cases were necessary or even useful. I realized that actually I felt the same – they aren't vital – but I did need my good idea to be recognized; I needed it not to be rubbished. I realized I was trying to be some sort of supermum, procuring every conceivable item for the good of the family. It was life-giving to realize that this wasn't a need I actually had. Deep down I didn't want or need to be that – those expectations came from somewhere else. So I could be released from these false needs. Untangling my feelings and needs helped me a great deal in making some adjustments in my approach to stressful domestic situations. Our needs won't always be met, of course, but I found I could be clearer about what they actually are and ask for the help I need. There are other times when, knowing my need, I mourn, because it cannot be met.

Having spurned the gift of a complete toothbrush holder, when given one after this incident, but before I had reflected on it, I'm now rather fond of my new one and I have noticed that other members of the family use these items too.

Self-empathy is extending to yourself the same compassion that you would seek to offer to someone else. We are called to love our neighbours as ourselves because each of us is made for love, and compassion increases through love. Our unmet needs are treasure to be unearthed, for they are a source of our healing.

- You may like to pay attention to a time when the strength of your reaction has surprised you or someone else and seek to be in touch with the feelings and needs that are underneath. It can be hard to name and connect with them. Imagining the situation with all your needs met can be a helpful way of connecting with what is missing.
- Buy yourself a toothbrush case?

Saturday: O Lord, open our lips

Blessed are you who weep now,
for you will laugh. (Luke 6.21)

O sing to the LORD a new song . . .
(Psalm 96.1)

You have kept count of my tossings;
put my tears in your bottle.
Are they not in your record?
(Psalm 56.8)

As a vicar in south London I often took funeral services for African and Caribbean Christians. These were big and long occasions with many tributes, and at the graveside there was singing while mourners took spades and filled in the grave. I was always moved by the warmth and the strength of a supportive community at these funerals. Sorrow could be expressed by tears, and comfort was gained by the fact that many were there who understood the depth of grief. They witnessed by their presence, and by their singing, to more than just a sense that life goes on: they showed that in God there is hope, and in the Church, love and support. On one occasion at the graveside the closest relative was struggling through her tears and the women there were looking to her to start off the singing. I felt for her and the pressure she seemed to be under, and I have always remembered the older woman who said to her, 'You must sing now; it is the source of your healing.'

Shock and trauma often numb and silence us. We can be aware of the deep emotions of grief and sorrow in us, even those pent up from the past, but be unable to express them. That is why we talk about the gift of tears, because tears signal the release of emotions. Crying is good for you and, having had a good cry for a time, at least there's an inner settling and a path forged, even if that next step is just to make a meal. When we've been silenced by adversity, an expression of healing is *finding our voice*. We often use the phrase to indicate a growth in confidence in someone.

Even if you don't consider yourself a good singer, you will be aware of your own voice and how your spoken voice stays the same throughout your life, making you easily recognizable to old friends and on the phone. In a choir, children, men and women have voices that enable them to sing particular parts. Our voices are personal and distinct, and can blend with the voices of others to produce harmony.

As a mother of choristers, I have often taken a fractious child to a choir practice, a child who is sullen or snappish and doesn't want to go. When I collect my son or daughter, I find a different creature. One of my children once said to me that she feels most in touch with who she really is when she sings. Perhaps that is why St Augustine said that the person who sings prays twice. What comes out of your mouth as you sing is very deeply part of yourself, taking you out of yourself. To sing requires a focus of mind, to manage words and music and breath. There's a deeper connection between us and the outside world than when we are speaking, for singing needs more breath and is louder than the spoken voice. We sing in worship because of this, and singing together is rousing and uplifting, a physical activity that resounds in our bodies and in the building. We also remember more easily what we have sung and find it can take us into the day and week.

To find your voice in a place of sorrow, and sing at a funeral, can feel impossible, but when you do your voice has the capacity to draw on your emotions, expressing and shaping them. The choice of song is what directs your expression of sorrow perhaps, if you sing the blues, or it can express your hope for love.

African American spirituals are religious folksongs, sung by slaves in earlier centuries as a powerful expression of their own voice, dignity, faith and solidarity with one another. They functioned as work songs to keep everyone in time, as well as an encouragement of faith in God and also coded messages of hope for escape. The spirituals kept the human spirit alive and open to a different, hopeful future.

Throughout the psalms we hear the invitation to sing a new song to the Lord. The invitation is to actually sing, to find and use your voice to express what is in your heart to God. In the psalms, which are full of emotions and direct speech to God, the song can be of anger or complaint; it can also be joy and praise. Singing a new song to the Lord involves engaging your voice, your breath and body. A song to the Lord is any song, sung in God's presence, offered to God for him to receive and draw you towards him. In this process, you express yourself more authentically and can hone your own voice.

As you come through adversity, more accepting of your own story and voice, or your needs and the grace of God, a new song will emerge. Singing itself will draw you out of where you have been, by the using of your voice, which is the source of your healing, but you need a new song to sing. The invitation is to sing something *new*; perhaps it is praise or gratitude and a new song rather than a cracked record. In the traditional sung services of the Anglican Church there are passages of Scripture that have been chosen to be sung daily, such as the Magnificat, a song of praise Mary probably already knew and sang, having been visited by the angel Gabriel. This canticle is sung at Evensong, where the response to the first words 'O Lord, open thou our lips' is 'And our mouth shall show forth thy praise' (Psalm 51.15). To sing before the Lord is a gift of God as well as a gift to God, an offering or sacrifice of praise.

Singing God's praises expresses our gratitude to God and reminds us of his faithfulness and steadfast love. Singing carries and our voices are heard beyond where we are. Our songs can invite accompaniment and modulation so others can join in. Voices that witness to a God of love and cry out for justice for all people need to be heard in our world. O Lord, open our lips.

- Choose a hymn, spiritual or song to sing or listen to, a song that could express some new insight or direction for this time in your life.

FRUITFUL: THE FIFTH WEEK

You prepare a table before me
in the presence of my enemies;
you anoint my head with oil;
my cup overflows.
(Psalm 23.5)

Having come through difficulty of some sort it is easy to take stock and say, 'Phew, I'm glad that's over; now I can get on with my life.' Adversity, however, changes us and we cannot go back to our life in the same way as before. We may remain stuck for a time, having gritted our teeth and got through, but still not able, long after the coping stage, to let our emotions catch up. It is never too late to grow through our difficult experiences to a deeper place of strengthening. For resilient people, there is a direction of growth that started in adversity and leads to altruism. It involves an openness to others, self-acceptance and a growing in compassion and wisdom. One may never be able to say that the subsequent experiences of kindness and light made the adversity worthwhile or justified it, but nevertheless out of it fruit has emerged. The kind of fruit that emerges often leads people to enter the caring professions or volunteer in work that enables them to give back in some way. This may be out of gratitude for having been helped and it may be using particular skills learned in times of difficulty. The fruit is seen in personal qualities. St Paul describes these as the fruit of the Spirit, which are 'love, joy, peace, patience, kindness, generosity, faithfulness, gentleness, and self-control'(Galatians 5.22–23).

The fruitfulness that has come from the experience of adversity, like the fruit of a tree, is part of a repeated natural, if not annual, cycle. Other parts of the cycle include times when there is battling to do with the wind and storms, perhaps of anxiety or conflict, and seasons where nothing much seems to happen. The strengthening gained by a resilient disciple bears fruit in compassion and wisdom. The disciple will still need pruning and will continue to encounter adversity. Deeper and more seasoned faith draws on the memory of having come through before by God's faithfulness and grace and enables trust in the present and for the future. The psalmist still experiences the enemies all around, but also God, not just providing what is needed, but anointing and blessing him too. Very often the external circumstances of our lives cannot be changed and we have to bear the hardship. Bereavement is an obvious example of this. We cannot be rescued or liberated. We cannot be saved from our situation, but we can be saved in it, and thus the quality of our life is different. We heal and become more whole in such a way that our interactions bring about healing more widely and for others.

Prayers for the week

For morning

As we rejoice in the gift of this new day,
so may the light of your presence, O God,
set our hearts on fire with love for you;
now and for ever.
(Opening prayer for Morning Prayer
from *Common Worship: Daily Prayer*)

For evening

Watch, dear Lord, with those who wake or weep tonight,
and let your angels protect those who sleep.
Tend the sick. Refresh the weary. Sustain the dying.
Calm the suffering. Pity the distressed.
We ask this for your love's sake.
(St Augustine of Hippo, 354–430)

Hymn

O Jesus, I have promised
To serve Thee to the end;
Be Thou forever near me,
My Master and my Friend;
I shall not fear the battle
If Thou art by my side,
Nor wander from the pathway
If Thou wilt be my Guide.

Oh, let me feel Thee near me;
The world is ever near;
I see the sights that dazzle,
The tempting sounds I hear;
My foes are ever near me,
Around me and within;
But, Jesus, draw Thou nearer,
And shield my soul from sin.

Oh, let me hear Thee speaking
In accents clear and still,
Above the storms of passion,
The murmurs of self-will;
Oh, speak to reassure me,
To hasten, or control;
Oh, speak, and make me listen,
Thou Guardian of my soul.

O Jesus, Thou hast promised
To all who follow Thee
That where Thou art in glory
There shall Thy servant be;
And Jesus, I have promised
To serve Thee to the end;
Oh, give me grace to follow,
My Master and my Friend.

Oh, let me see Thy footmarks
And in them plant mine own;
My hope to follow duly
Is in Thy strength alone.
Oh, guide me, call me, draw me,
Uphold me to the end;
And then to rest receive me,
My Saviour and my Friend.
(John Bode, 1816–74)

Words from Scripture

For in Christ Jesus neither circumcision nor uncircumcision counts for anything; the only thing that counts is faith working through love. (Galatians 5.6)

You will know them by their fruits. (Matthew 7.20)

Abide in me as I abide in you. Just as the branch cannot bear fruit by itself unless it abides in the vine, neither can you unless you abide in me. I am the vine, you are the branches. Those who abide in me and I in them bear much fruit, because apart from me you can do nothing. (John 15.4–5)

A psalm to read

Psalm 100

Monday: success without swords

> But Peter said, 'I have no silver or gold, but what I have I give you; in the name of Jesus Christ of Nazareth, stand up and walk.' (Acts 3.6)

> Yet more than ever believers were added to the Lord, great numbers of both men and women, so that they even carried out the sick into the streets, and laid them on cots and mats, in order that Peter's shadow might fall on some of them as he came by. (Acts 5.14–15)

After the Ascension and Pentecost, we see Peter taking the lead. The band of disciples grew, in just a few chapters in the book of the Acts of the Apostles, into a movement. As we see how Peter has developed, we might be inclined to think that his discipleship looks like a naive 'before' and a successful 'after'. But Peter is a disciple who matures and grows in resilience all the way through his life, from his call by Lake Galilee to his crucifixion in Rome under the emperor Nero, reportedly upside down, him not being worthy, he said, of being crucified the same way as Jesus.

The movement Peter leads grows in numbers and so we could judge him as a great success. Being a resilient disciple is less about success, however, than about strength and the capacity to meet the challenges in our path with wisdom and compassion. The strength is not that of being invincible or unaffected by external circumstances but of being mature enough to continue to develop and change in response to them. Peter grows into a wise leader, the principal pastor, and from this comes the tradition that he became the bishop of Rome, the first pope. Once the one who jostled to prove himself, be there first and lead, we now see Peter leading with others and for the good of all. He manages to deal first with a variety of community concerns such as finding a replacement for Judas, appointing deacons to ensure that Greek- and Hebrew-speaking widows were provided for equally (Acts 6.1–7) and uncovering the lies told by Ananias and Sapphira about the money they gave to the Church (Acts 5.1–12).

These problems arose because of the success of the Church. The numbers grew and so organization became complex. Peter's skills grew accordingly and he became the steady rock Jesus predicted he would be, a pillar of the early Church. Success for a church leader or pastor isn't about numbers, though there is a great deal of pressure on churches and clergy to focus on them as the primary measure of growth in Christ. The health of a church is expressed in whether the flock, under the leadership of the shepherd, find comfort, their souls restored, a lack of fear and the presence of goodness and mercy – the qualities found in Psalm 23.

I often take part in services that celebrate the arrival of a new vicar. I generally give the new person a card and I often write that I hope and pray that this new ministry will be a blessing to them as well as to those they serve. Following Jesus should bring about flourishing for the disciple, not leave them worn out. Sometimes we may look only for the following and the fruit in our leaders and forget the importance of flourishing for them. The reality of both falling and the faithfulness of God is true for every disciple, though there are times when we can resent vulnerability or failure in our leaders, failing to be Christ to them. Leading a church is a demanding call, and when leaders and members are able and willing to share of themselves and discover their own gifts all can flourish.

Those who are resilient, who have come through some adversity, often report that a sense of vulnerability and anxiety emerges from time to time, as well as sometimes finding it difficult to trust others. As we learn more about trauma, we know too that there can be flashbacks and depression. Peter is a resilient disciple because the direction of his travel indicates his own flourishing, despite new difficulties. He became a powerful preacher and was constantly retelling the story of the death and resurrection of Jesus, a story with violence and brutality, and one in which he did not shine. He was only able to do this because he had reframed the story of the denials and death with the reality of a resurrection life that transforms at the deepest level. It would also keep him humble.

That Peter also became someone who could heal others indicates the way in which he was able to bring his own experience of woundedness into play when others needed healing, in themselves or in their relationships. Peter had taken a sword to Malchus in the garden of Gethsemane in an attempt to serve Jesus. Jesus had healed the ear and in this and in rising from the dead had shown Peter that following his way would involve trusting God to bring about new life, discerning the time to let go and no longer fight. Jesus had told Peter long before that he would be given the keys of the kingdom, a kingdom not of this world. These keys do not open worldly treasure but unlock the way to God, by freeing lives and hearts. Peter understood this, saying to the man he healed at the Temple gate, 'I do not have silver or gold to give you, but what I have I give you.' We hear of Peter raising Tabitha from the dead in a similar way to Jesus when he raised Jairus's daughter (Acts 9.36–42; Mark 5.21–43). Peter becomes the successor of Jesus in trusting God to bring life from death.

Humility is the quality that Peter developed and all mature Christians grow into, a quality where a deep sense of inner dignity and value is palpable to others and brings them solace. It is a fruit of the Spirit, sometimes translated as 'gentleness'. It can be misunderstood as a false modesty of doing yourself down and as such can be quite manipulative, in refusing to allow others to express gratitude or admiration, for example. Humble people are grounded (which means lowly, on the ground or earth). They are secure in themselves and in touch with their own vulnerability, as human beings but also fully aware of their strengths. Humility enables someone to extend hospitality to another, creating a safe space where someone else's needs and strengths can be recognized. When you are confident of your own place in the world, not struggling to prove yourself or be recognized, you can be free to take an interest in and bring out the best in others. In humility you can see the vulnerabilities of another and generously use your knowledge to support, guide and affirm that person. A humble approach to others unlocks gifts for the good of a household or a church community and brings about reconciliation and peace in fractious circumstances. It is an inner quality that comes from those who are secure, mature and able to be generous with themselves.

- Is there something you could say to a particular church leader or fellow Christian, or something you could do for that person, that would recognize his or her humanity and need to flourish?
- After Easter read the book of the Acts of the Apostles and trace the maturing and fruitfulness of the earliest Christians.

Tuesday: thin places

> The voice said to Peter again, a second time, 'What God has made clean, you must not call profane.' This happened three times, and the thing was suddenly taken up to heaven. (Acts 10.15–16)

> While Peter was still speaking, the Holy Spirit fell upon all who heard the word. The circumcised believers who had come with Peter were astounded that the gift of the Holy Spirit had been poured out even on the Gentiles, for they heard them speaking in tongues and extolling God. Then Peter said, 'Can anyone withhold the water for baptizing these people who have received the Holy Spirit just as we have?' So he ordered them to be baptized in the name of Jesus Christ. Then they invited him to stay for several days. (Acts 10.44–48)

There is a Celtic saying that states heaven and earth are only three feet apart, but in 'thin places' that distance is even shorter. The ancient pagan Celts and the Christians after them described particular places, especially wild ones, such as the island of Iona, as thin places. Such a place is where the veil that separates heaven and earth is lifted and you are able to receive a glimpse of the glory of God. Sometimes it is a place that is thin, or sacred. The thin and well-worn place of a garment shows you that you kneel a lot or put your elbows on the table. On a teddy bear the thin place reveals the contours of love and attachment.

Sometimes it is the way rather than the place – the way in which an experience echoes with our own history causes us to pay attention. As we notice patterns, we can experience an invitation to do something great, to live beyond the bounds of ourselves and participate in the greater good, or the life of God in the world. As we grow in resilience we cannot but express the adversities of the past except in altruism. Healed and restored, our empathy increases and we share the love and freedom with others. We see this in Peter's life.

Peter experiences a thin place where he can recognize well-worn patterns for glimpsing God in his life. He pays attention, follows the inner prompting, and because he does he plays a huge role in changing the course of early Christianity. It goes from being a religion for Jews to being a faith that accepted Gentiles and their lifestyle and thus a worldwide movement. This comes about for Peter because of a vision that resonated with his experiences of his own life and God's work in it. One of the experiences that he drew on was of the well-worn pattern of three in his life. Another was the time on Mount Tabor, where Peter, along with James and John, had glimpsed Jesus, transfigured. They had climbed up the high mountain to pray and then had this vision of Jesus, radiant, standing with Moses and Elijah (Luke 9.28–36). There was a voice from heaven that said, 'This is my Son, my Chosen; listen to him.' It wasn't until after the resurrection that these disciples spoke about the event and what it meant.

After the resurrection and Pentecost, Peter had a third experience that came three times and, as in the previous ones of denying he knew Jesus three times and Jesus asking him three times if he loved him, Peter is again changed. He was travelling at the time and had stopped in Joppa. He stayed with Simon the tanner and went on to the roof to pray. Now Peter was tired and hungry, but he was open to God up on the roof and he had a vision that he didn't understand immediately, but knew was important. Peter saw a tablecloth being lowered to the ground with animals in it that Jews were forbidden to eat. A voice told him to kill and eat them but he refused, replying that he had never eaten anything unclean. This vision and voice was repeated three times and Peter was bemused. Perhaps he was just hungry, but he knew that anything happening three times had significance for him and he had had visions and heard God's voice before. The roof of a house of a tanner, traditionally an unclean occupation (it being necessary to work with the leather), isn't noted as being a thin place in which to glimpse God. The voice, though, told him three times not to call unclean what God had created.

Visitors arrived, saying that their Gentile master Cornelius had had a vision that he should send for Peter to come. So Peter went, cautious about going to a Gentile household, but mindful of his mysterious vision and also intrigued that the centurion Cornelius had also had a vision. Peter tells Cornelius and his household about Jesus and it is clear that they received the Holy Spirit, even though they hadn't become Jews. So Peter, convinced this was of God, baptized them. Peter had glimpsed God on the roof, without understanding what it meant, and then he glimpsed God being experienced directly by Gentiles, those he once thought were far from God and unclean.

The story of Peter's threefold vision and the conversion of Cornelius is less well known than the story of Peter denying Jesus three times. Perhaps we are more interested in Peter falling and then knowing he was restored than with realizing that when he and we are restored it is to live more deeply and compassionately. If we pretend we haven't got things wrong or been vulnerable in any way we will miss the thin places in which we glimpse God and experience love itself, for ourselves and to share with others. Peter remembers the threes, remembers that sometimes you don't know and need to ponder and pray for a while, despite now being a respected church leader to whom others look for guidance. Our lives will bear fruit for ourselves and others when we continue to know we are vulnerable and our souls before God are thin enough to glimpse God. Our wounds, now healed, can be put to the service of others. Here we see Peter as an evangelist catching a new set of people, as Jesus originally called him to be, and as pastor or shepherd, gathering and teaching a new flock. His life has come full circle.

The good news of Jesus Christ, Peter realized, having preached to Cornelius and his household, included the fact that God can be experienced directly, anywhere and by everyone. Peter then argued for the inclusion of Gentiles in the Church. Peter took time to pray, time to remember, reflect and relate. Our hearts, minds and relationships are thin places in which we glimpse God. This will always result in crossing barriers and including others who are different from us. When we pray we are open to God and when we love we are open to one another. Saints are those who have become a thin place where others can glimpse God.

- Call to mind a thin place where you have glimpsed God. Can you go to a physical place in your imagination and allow it to refresh you?
- Is there a well-worn pattern to pay attention to, one that invites you to live beyond yourself in some way?

Wednesday: abiding to be fruitful

> I am the true vine, and my Father is the vine-grower. He removes every branch in me that bears no fruit. Every branch that bears fruit he prunes to make it bear more fruit. (John 15.1–2)

> So we have known and believe the love that God has for us. God is love, and those who abide in love abide in God, and God abides in them. (1 John 4.16)

The white blossom of apple trees and the pinks of cherry blossom show us that spring is underway. After the bare rough branches of winter such delicate flowers are a joy to see. The pale colours are appropriate to such fragile flowers that are often dashed to the ground by wind and rain. The petals don't last long, but they are signs of hope for the tree, making possible pollination by insects, animals or human beings.

When the blossom has gone, the serious business of growing full leaves gets underway. In the period of flowering, however, when petals can open to the sun, we see that the tree lives and know that it will bear fruit in time.

When we comment that a person is blossoming, we mean that there is a new confidence or attractiveness about them. It is not that the speaker is surprised, but pleased, and there is a sense of needing to nurture, protect and celebrate such growth for it to continue and become a permanent feature of someone's life. When we have come through a time of change there is a period of feeling the vitality of newness but testing ourselves and our capabilities cautiously. We do this with the spring weather in the UK by carrying our umbrellas and sunglasses as we dodge the April showers. We 'ne'er cast a clout 'til May is out', which I understand to mean that we don't put our winter clothes away until the May blossom has come out. There can be setbacks to the onset of spring and when we open a new chapter of life, and it is wise to make sure we have the equivalent protection of a woolly jumper and a mac in place until we are more confident of the territory when we venture forth.

The beauty of spring is not the end of all the winter weather, and indeed spring itself is short and fragile. For growth to continue and for there to be fruit, pollination, warmth and rain are needed, and then patience while time and nature make growth happen. The direction of the growth cycle of a plant or tree is towards fruitfulness. In human life this is also true with the fruit of the Spirit lived out.

Jesus, in describing himself as the True Vine, his disciples as the branches and God the Father as the vine-grower, points to the importance of time, firm intervention and the patience of abiding as necessary for a human being to be fruitful spiritually. It is the branches abiding in the true vine that ensures fruitfulness. When we can't 'abide' something, we won't have anything to do with it. To abide in Christ, as branches abide in a vine, means being close, connected, sharing the same sap or life-force, and being content to remain. This most naturally happens in prayer and worship, in paying attention and in love.

We can often think of Christian discipleship as something very busy. Indeed, some of us are very active in church trying to get people to go on rotas to get things done, and busy with fundraising and important good works that make a real difference to people's lives. Sometimes this can get out of kilter and distract us from being in the presence of God in worship or it can even smack of seeking to earn our salvation. Jesus asked Martha why she was so distracted by all that needed to be done when she could be sitting with him and her sister Mary (Luke 10.38–42).

Abiding in Christ involves praying in a way that enables us to know we are accepted by God, forgiven, healed and strengthened to walk in newness of life. Such being at home in ourselves and in the presence of God enables us to cope with the uncertainties and changes that come with life. A vine is trained to grow across a trellis so that space is created for the bunches of grapes to grow. Taking the time and space to abide in Christ enables creativity and a lessening of anxiety that helps us cope with the trials and tribulations of life. Jesus describes these as the pruning that fruitful branches have to undergo, under the care of the vine-grower.

Pruning brings about growth. To grow, the branches of the True Vine have to be pruned. Some branches are lopped off, some are cut back, some are trimmed, all in the service of growth. When our lives are pruned in some way it can be a relief. We can value a little trimming, though small put-downs can be hard to bear perhaps, especially if they contain the kind of truth that can help us grow more mature. More major chopping back can take various forms and can be necessary. We can become unbalanced, overgrown in some skills or experiences, which demands a cutting back and a focusing of energy elsewhere. One of the signs of wisdom or maturity is the ability to cope with the emotional pain of regular pruning and the recognition that it is part of life.

The bunches of grapes are what the vine is all about. Fruit is not an end in itself for the vine, however; it is the means by which a plant reproduces itself. In Christian terms that is mission and evangelism. For the vine-grower, it is the grapes that are the purpose of the work and what they will be used for. We take grapes to hospital bedsides to aid healing; we put them in lunch boxes or bowls to remind us to eat healthily or on a plate to paint them, to appreciate the beauty of creation in a still life. You will have to decide whether the fruit of your discipleship brings healing, sustains the health of the whole or is purely decorative. To seek to abide in Christ, the True Vine, acknowledges the fact that growth will be forged through the changes that come with pruning, as well as the rest and safety that come with abiding in Christ.

We also grow vines, of course, to use the grapes for wine. The vocation of the grape, pressed and fermented over time, involves complete transformation. It is the fruit that reveals to us the sacrifice of Christ. His sacrifice, the pain he bore, we commemorate as we 'Do this in remembrance' of him and experience the foretaste of a heavenly banquet with a vintage in which all can find the hope of salvation.

- Consider where the blossom is in your life and in the life of your church and how you might protect and nurture it.
- Where is spiritual growth to be seen in you, and what pruning back or lopping off will enable the growth?
- Abide in prayer. You could slowly say the words 'Be still and know that I am God', several times, and then reduce the sentence to 'Be still and know', 'Be still' and then 'Be'.

Thursday: Peter and Paul

> When [Paul] had come to Jerusalem, he attempted to join the disciples; and they were all afraid of him, for they did not believe that he was a disciple. But Barnabas took him, brought him to the apostles, and described for them how on the road he had seen the Lord, who had spoken to him, and how in Damascus he had spoken boldly in the name of Jesus. (Acts 9.26–27)

> But when I saw that they were not acting consistently with the truth of the gospel, I said to Cephas before them all, 'If you, though a Jew, live like a Gentile and not like a Jew, how can you compel the Gentiles to live like Jews?' (Galatians 2.14)

> You are the salt of the earth; but if salt has lost its taste, how can its saltiness be restored? It is no longer good for anything, but is thrown out and trampled under foot. (Matthew 5.13)

The pressure to be nice can be quite compelling for a Christian. Jesus called us to be salt of the earth, and although it is true that at first glance it looks almost identical to sugar they are quite different, in tea, for example. Salt preserves both the freshness and the distinctive flavours of food. Sugar makes food taste nice, makes it palatable. A culture of niceness has the effect of creating distance in the relationships in a community. So fearful are we of rocking the boat or offending, we cease to show interest in others. In thinking that being nice is more important than sharing our concerns or irritations in a relationship, we can store up problems that, though once small, get bigger and laced with bitterness. Churches can fall into a niceness that is a pale shadow of kindness, and far removed from genuine love. Perhaps nowhere is this more obvious in attitudes towards conflict and disagreement that are seen as negative and to be avoided, or done away with quickly.

Conflict and disagreement are normal aspects of human relating. They arise because of the rich diversity of human experience and expression. When we allow ourselves and others the freedom to express their thoughts and feelings, giving time and attention, the relationships are deepened, creative and fruitful. The early Christians found themselves in conflict. The central issue was whether Christ had saved Gentiles by his death and resurrection, or only Gentiles who became Jews and lived by the Jewish law. It wasn't just a matter of individually held opinions, because it had an impact on what food people ate. Eating together was essential at the Lord's Supper or Communion, and for fellowship. We see in the pages of the New Testament some of the story of this dispute and the way in which Peter and Paul worked through it, practically, theologically and with each other. Over many years there was what we might call a holy confusion and a struggle for blessing.

Peter and Paul represented Jewish and Gentile Christians. Both sought to be faithful to Christ and to the experience of the Holy Spirit in the communities that they pastored. We know the end of that bit of the story. Christians do not keep Jewish food laws, but there are always other similar struggles to have one's identity as a Christian acknowledged and accepted. Christians throughout history have lived in very different ways and come from diverse cultures and they still do. These differences challenge us to see and serve Christ in each person and to thrash out the arguments and implications in a way that honours Christ's body, the Church. In the contemporary Church it is issues to do with race, gender and sexuality that challenge us, because the lines of who we have seen as Christian or what it takes to lead are being redrawn – and differently in different places. What hasn't changed is the presence of the Holy Spirit to open our hearts to others and to what is new for us, or the demands and difficulty of conflict.

As in so many disagreements it isn't just about the issue itself. There were personal and generational dynamics that both Peter and Paul had to attend to in the conflict about how to include Gentiles as Christians. Though Peter and Paul were both Jewish, they were quite different from each other, representing different cultures and social backgrounds. Peter was a fisherman from Galilee, had known Jesus and had been given the leadership of the Church. He welcomed the inclusion of Gentiles, ate whatever he was served when with them, but when he was with Jewish Christians, aware that they continued to keep the food laws, he did so too. Paul thought that this was hypocritical, that it undermined the inclusion of Gentiles, and he told him so publicly. Now Paul was an educated Jew, born in Syria, Greek-speaking, well-travelled and a Roman citizen. His public status carried weight in the world. Unlike Peter, he hadn't known Jesus, but his encounter with the risen Christ on the road to Damascus had changed him from persecuting Christians to becoming the apostle to the Gentiles.

It isn't difficult to see how these two men could be at loggerheads, but despite difference, their convictions were shared and their actions and decisions enabled Gentiles to be Christians. Peter didn't see Paul as an upstart, come to change the religious practices of the Church and upset everything with new thinking. Peter had not just one key, but the keys of the kingdom, and the unlocking of the way to God needed many forms. He was gracious and far-sighted, enabling Paul to be trusted as a new, but feared, Christian and then to take his place in the Church. In the contemporary Church we have developed 'fresh expressions' of church, different from inherited church models. There are some who would undermine the idea of a church in a café, or café style, fearing perhaps that their own church is being criticized or under threat.

Peter doesn't stop being a Jewish Christian, but he is able to bless and encourage the ministry of those taking the gospel further than he would ever go. He made way for the next generation of the Church. Mentoring others for roles to come is a mark of a mature Christian. Barnabas has an important role in bridging the two communities and the two pillars that are Peter and Paul. There are times when we are wise to have a mediator or mutually trusted person to help us bridge differences. Conflict can more easily be transformed into a creative process where each person is able to see that he or she has a special role to follow in the service of all. As salt we will draw out the distinctiveness and preserve the goodness in our relating.

Christians are called to hospitality rather than tolerance and that demands quite a deep understanding of people as groups as individuals, the forging of real connections between everyone who comes and everyone we want to reach with the good news of God's love. All this is part of mission and evangelism, integral aspects of what it means to be Christ's body, the Church. It takes different forms in different places, but has been expressed as what are commonly called the 'five marks of mission'. Mission expressed as Tell, Teach,

Tend, Treasure the earth and Transform society is the fruit of the good news of Jesus Christ.

- How might you create a hospitable space to listen to the difference between you and someone else?
- Which of the five marks of mission are clearly seen in your church, which are hidden and which need to emerge?

Friday: out of kilter

> You will not fear the terror of the night,
> or the arrow that flies by day,
> or the pestilence that stalks in darkness,
> or the destruction that wastes at noonday.
> (Psalm 91.5–6)

> Martha, Martha, you are worried and distracted by many things; there is need of only one thing. (Luke 10.41)

A. A. Milne wrote *The House at Pooh Corner* in 1928 and has delighted generations with his stories about Winne the Pooh and his friends. In the story titled 'In which Rabbit has a busy day, and we learn what Christopher Robin does in the mornings', we find that Rabbit has woken up knowing that something 'Important' is going to occur, and that he is going to organize, or lead, or bring order out of chaos. It is the kind of day that involves the other animals saying 'Yes, Rabbit' and 'No, Rabbit' at intervals, and letting him tell them what to do.

I notice in myself a tendency, at times of stress, to continue being busy, continue working, or just to make that last phone call of the day in a way that is somehow driven. In Rabbit the busyness seems to be driven by his need to be seen to be important and capable. In me, mostly, it is driven by a need to keep at bay the feeling of being weary, anxious or exhausted. It is easier to keep going than to stop and realize that I'm tired and should withdraw to rest, to pray and to realign myself. It's a time when I am likely to complain to members of my household that they should be clearing things up in the house and being more supportive.

The description of Rabbit is not unlike the description of the monk suffering under the vice of acedia, which we read of in the work of the fourth-century monk John Cassian and others. Acedia, or accidie, is the vice of the noonday demon of Psalm 91. Its old name is sloth, but there are two manifestations of this vice that work against the virtue of fortitude, or what we might call resilience. Rabbit is a busybody and Cassian describes some monks as busybodies, those who, affected by acedia, are driven from their cells in a way that is unstable and feckless, and become trapped in the affairs, harmful concerns and business of others. Such monks can apparently undertake virtuous activities such as charitable work or caring for the sick but to the wrong measure and with the wrong motivation. The monk in this condition is in danger of using other people in order to feel good about himself, and avoiding remaining in his cell feeling he is making no spiritual progress. In addition to being driven to go visiting, the monk is prone to feeling superior and critical of the failings of others. He believes the community has become unspiritual and uncompassionate so that there is no one to console him.

When drawn to the vice of acedia, it may not be a drive to help others and interfere that comes to the fore as it does with Rabbit, but something more akin to the lifestyle of a sloth. It is easy to picture a sloth creeping very slowly, upside down along a branch, stopping to sleep, frequently. Acedia causes the monk to sleep in the afternoon and not attend to making spiritual progress. Sometimes the vice is described as laziness, burnout or boredom. A person affected can swing from superiority to self-denigration, and avoids self-awareness and self-care by sleep or distraction.

Acedia is a spiritual carelessness. It is important to recognize the times when we are avoiding ourselves and God. When we have come through difficulty it is natural to be not only grateful but also relieved that the past is behind us. We can be bored of what we can think of as navel-gazing and reluctant to own our own story. We need, however, to take care of ourselves and attend to the cycles of our own healing. This does not mean pampering ourselves, though there may be times for that, or letting ourselves off the hook. It means examining our motivations and discerning what we need in order to flourish. When we seek to give back out of gratitude for what we have been given, we can sometimes so cherish the feeling of being the giver that we forget we need to receive, not only from God but also from others. We are impoverished if we do not have relationships of mutuality, and in some walks of life, such as the caring professions, or family roles, it can be difficult to feel able to receive. Being able to give of ourselves and to give back in gratitude for what we have received is an important part of being human.

We find invitations to repair, heal and give as new cycles of our life come round. Aware of Jesus' words that it is more blessed to give than to receive (Acts 20.35), we can, however, get out of balance and avoid meeting or even noticing our own needs. Without receiving care we are out of kilter personally. We also do not care well for others.

The golden rule of ethics is: 'In everything do to others as you would have them do to you; for this is the law and the prophets' (Matthew 7.12). For those who more commonly neglect meeting their own needs, because they have been taught that it is selfish or some other reason, it can take time to discover what care to give to oneself and what care to offer to others. One can feel rejected personally because someone needs something different from what we'd like to give. It is then that we have a chance to work out the balance of our need to give and another's to receive. Sheryl Sandberg in her book, *Option B: Facing adversity, building resilience, and finding joy*, talks of learning the Platinum Rule of friendship. This is a decision to treat people as they want to be treated. It goes beyond self-awareness to empathy and to taking the cue from someone else.

Being a busybody like Rabbit or lazy like a sloth are two alternative responses to sensing some cycle of inner work has returned for us to attend to and avoiding it. The journey of spiritual growth continues, and in the presence of God we can be held as we remember what has been and have compassion on ourselves. It is out of God's love for us that we can love ourselves and others. We need to notice and watch out for the two aspects of the vice of acedia in order to continue on the narrow road of developing resilience. Once we are aware and alert to tendencies that will derail us, it is the cultivation of the virtue or quality of discernment that will hone the decisions we make so that our path is life-giving.

- Is it busyness or coming to a standstill that you see yourself as having a tendency towards when it comes to avoiding something important in your life, like your own well-being?
- What care do you need for yourself, or to offer to another?

Saturday: angels

> Suddenly an angel of the Lord appeared and a light shone in the cell. He tapped Peter on the side and woke him, saying, 'Get up quickly.' And the chains fell off his wrists. The angel said to him, 'Fasten your belt and put on your sandals.' He did so. Then he said to him, 'Wrap your cloak around you and follow me.' Peter went out and followed him; he did not realize that what was happening with the angel's help was real; he thought he was seeing a vision. (Acts 12.7–9)

> Rejoice always, pray without ceasing, give thanks in all circumstances; for this is the will of God in Christ Jesus for you.
> (1 Thessalonians 5.16–18)

In the 1987 German film *Wings of Desire* two angels glide through the streets of Berlin, able to hear the inner sorrows of the human population. They provide hope, invisibly, and we see them in black and white, the way in which they see the world. We observe them put a hand on someone's back or hold close someone just about to jump off a high building. This moving film speaks to the ways in which our hearts and motivation can rise and fall and we can't really point to why. The comfort the actions of these angels bring is felt by the distressed human, and their actual presence is perceived by just a few; but as spirits they do not interact with people, that is, of course, until one falls in love . . .

Peter, leading the church in Jerusalem, experienced opposition and persecution that involved a threat to his life and to that of the emerging Church. Just because you have come through once doesn't mean facing a new challenge is easy; indeed it can make you more aware of what it will cost. The early Church suffered because the apostles were no longer afraid of what the authorities could do to them and so preached openly. Crucifixion had not got rid of Jesus. But there was still fear, which we see in the cautious way in which Paul was received as a convert. Persecution is not to be sought, or pain courted, though it often comes to people who know who they are and what they stand for.

Peter was arrested under the orders of King Herod because Herod had gained in popularity when he had had James, Jesus' brother, killed by the sword. It was Passover and the political situation was as tense and unpredictable as it had been the year Jesus had been executed. No longer imprisoned by a fear of what might happen to him, Peter had an inner freedom, even though the keys of the kingdom did not extend to being able to open a cell. The highly practical angel took care of that, providing light to see, getting him dressed and then telling him, 'Wrap your cloak around you and follow me.' But then he was left and had to find his own way to a Christian household, and in an encounter that echoes both the resurrection and the walking on the water, Rhoda isn't believed when she says she has opened the door to Peter and she is told she has seen a ghost.

Resilient discipleship and resurrection life, it is clear, do not lessen the difficulties that come, but they are met with an awareness of the presence of those who will help, the whole company of heaven. Some helpers will be unseen, supporting by their prayer, which will have real effects. Some of the unseen, or only just glimpsed, will be angels, messengers of God who will bring practical help of the heart as well as help in the physical world. As we grow in wisdom and compassion we are often much more conscious of the small acts of kindness and goodness that become the turning points in people's lives and of the fact that the way in which things are done is as important as what is done, if it is to have any purchase. Awareness of the close proximity of God frees us to trust that God will prompt, hold and complete our endeavours. Peter was left outside by the angel, but his release had come about in a partnership – between an angel, Peter's ability to think and act, and the Christians at Mary's house who would hide and advise, at no small cost to themselves. If we restrict our view of angels to fairy godmothers granting wishes, we will find life less beautiful and joyful than it is when we pray constantly, rejoice and give thanks, open to the ladder of partnership between heaven and earth.

That well-grounded and wise mystic, Mother Julian of Norwich, encourages us to approach life hopefully, with a deep knowledge of God's care and keeping of us, by her words, 'All will be well and all manner of things will be well.' This is not naive optimism but a Christian hopefulness for the details of life's journey, not just the cosmic victory won. It enables us to face the day with hope, work for justice with courage, and trust in the seen and unseen work of God constantly present.

- Are there invisible walls within you that imprison and divide and might there be angels to help free you from them?
- Spend some time in prayer for the day to come. Where would an angel inspire you, comfort you and guide you in what will be?

FULFIL: HOLY WEEK

Traditionally, Christian congregations hear in church the whole of the Passion story on Palm Sunday but do not read as far as the resurrection. This comes after a Palm Sunday procession that sets the tone for us, entering into the week as a journey, participating as if we were those first disciples. This happens in various ways in churches during the week. Some churches gather to eat a Passover meal. Many will go to church on Maundy Thursday; some of us will have our feet washed at the service. We might stay on that night so that we watch for one hour or longer. Congregations often leave silently, scattering like the disciples did then and on Good Friday. Many get up before dawn on Easter Day to wait in the darkness and then to greet the risen Christ.

The focus of this week is on Jesus as the one who fulfils his vocation to save, reconcile, bring peace and atone. We have prayed with the theme of struggle, through which we have sought to grow and mature, by the grace of God. We have reflected on ourselves and our relationships in order to grow stronger in our inner life and to live out this strengthening by wisdom and compassion. Jesus is the pattern for us on this journey of resilience. In this week, in him, we see the perfect example of facing adversity. We see him, truly human, struggle and suffer, seek support and be betrayed. We see him follow a path that, before it takes him to life, leads him through death. This death enables humanity thereafter to flourish and be fruitful, confident that in Christ life comes out of death, light out of darkness and hope from despair.

The suffering of Christ is costly. We see Christ struggle, disappointed with his faithless disciples, in pain and in desperation. We see Christ get to places of calm where he can totally trust God, show compassion to others who suffer, and forgive, even in the midst of betrayal and pain. Christ, in his divine humanity, really suffers. His humanity is whole and he can give himself in love to God and to the world. Christ's inner presence is what comes through, the inner unseen work of holiness and prayer that brings about change and shifts not only in those whom he encounters but also for the salvation of the world. We see Jesus as a pattern for our lives. He is centred and fully present in all that happens and he is able to bear the suffering and from within it bring about peace, healing and hope. At the right time, he surrenders to death and to God, and discovers that God is faithful and raises him from death to life.

Disciples of Jesus can be resilient because Jesus leads the way and accompanies us through adversity and into life. The strengthening is of the inner self and of love for God and for others. It comes through our struggles and prayers and the grace of God. We can surrender at the last, even, perhaps especially, in death, because we have seen and experienced that God is faithful.

As we enter this Holy Week you may wish to reflect particularly on the pattern that Jesus sets in the events of the week, the pattern that shows us the path through suffering and to life. In doing so, pray for the strength, wisdom and compassion into which God leads you, in order to join Christ in his work of redemption in the circumstances of your life.

Prayers for the week

For morning

I arise today
through God's mighty strength,
his power to uphold me,
his wisdom to guide me,
and his hand to guard me.

I arise today
through Christ's mighty strength,
through his death and resurrection,
through the Spirit's empowering,
through the presence of angels
and the love of the saints,
through the threefold Trinity
to protect me from evil.
(St Patrick, *c.*389–*c.*461)

For evening

Eternal God,
in the cross of Jesus
we see the cost of our sin
and the depth of your love:
in humble hope and fear
may we place at his feet
all that we have and all that we are,
through Jesus Christ our Lord.
(Additional collect for Good
Friday from *Common Worship*)

Hymn

Father, hear the prayer we offer:
Not for ease that prayer shall be,
But for strength that we may ever
Live our lives courageously.

Not for ever in green pastures
Do we ask our way to be;
But the steep and rugged pathway
May we tread rejoicingly.

Not for ever by still waters
Would we idly rest and stay;
But would smite the living fountains
From the rocks along our way.

Be our strength in hours of weakness,
In our wanderings be our guide;
Through endeavour, failure, danger,
Father, be thou at our side.
(Maria Willis, 1824–1908)

Hymn

O sacred head, sore wounded,
Defiled and put to scorn;
O kingly head, surrounded
With mocking crown of thorn:
What sorrow mars thy grandeur?
Can death thy bloom deflow'r?
O countenance whose splendour
The hosts of heav'n adore!

Thy beauty, long desired,
Hath vanished from our sight;
Thy pow'r is all expired,
And quenched the light of light.
Ah me! for whom thou diest,
Hide not so far thy grace:
Show me, O Love most highest,
The brightness of thy face.

I pray thee, Jesus, own me,
Me, Shepherd good, for thine;

Who to thy fold hast won me,
And fed with truth divine.
Me guilty, me refuse not,
Incline thy face to me,
This comfort that I lose not,
On earth to comfort thee.

In thy most bitter passion
My heart to share doth cry,
With thee for my salvation
Upon the cross to die.
Ah, keep my heart thus moved
To stand thy cross beneath,
To mourn thee, well-beloved,
Yet thank thee for thy death.

My days are few, O fail not,
With thine immortal pow'r,
To hold me that I quail not
In death's most fearful hour:
That I may fight befriended,
And see in my last strife
To me thine arms extended
Upon the cross of life.

(Paul Gerhardt, 1607–76,
from a fourteenth-century
Latin hymn, translated by
Robert Bridges, 1844–1930)

Words of Scripture

For God so loved the world that he gave his only Son, so that everyone who believes in him may not perish but may have eternal life.

(John 3.16)

Do this in remembrance of me. (Luke 22.19)

So if I, your Lord and Teacher, have washed your feet, you also ought to wash one another's feet. For I have set you an example, that you also should do as I have done to you. (John 13.14–15)

Monday: Hosanna

Ride on, ride on in majesty!
The winged squadrons of the sky
Look down with sad and wondering eyes
To see the approaching sacrifice.
(Henry Milman, 1791–1868)

> [Pilate] said to the Jews, 'Here is your King!' They cried out, 'Away with him! Away with him! Crucify him!' Pilate asked them, 'Shall I crucify your King?' The chief priests answered, 'We have no king but the emperor.' (John 19.14–15)

I have a very clear memory of waiting eagerly in the theatre for a production of *Jesus Christ Superstar* to begin. Then I suddenly realized I was going to have to go through the emotional roller coaster that makes up the events of Holy Week and I had to brace myself, decide to engage on a deeper level rather than just expect to be entertained. 'Do I really have to go through this again?' was my question. In the Palm Sunday hymn 'Ride on, ride on', it is the angels who 'look down with sad and wondering eyes' as they see Jesus enter Jerusalem on a donkey, for they can see the inevitable suffering that is to come. This week turns upside down our notions of what real power is and how it is held. It turns upside down our notions of how life-giving change is brought about and the role suffering plays in bringing about that life-giving change.

Crowds flocked to Jesus riding on a donkey. They waved palms and hailed him as king, crying 'Hosanna', 'Save us, deliver us', but his was not the only procession at the beginning of the big festival. The imperial army also entered Jerusalem, its cavalry and soldiers led by the governor Pontius Pilate. The army was there at Passover in case there was trouble but also to show the dominance of Roman power. Passover, of course, was when the Jews were celebrating Israel's deliverance from slavery in Egypt. The people again wanted deliverance, but this time from the Romans, and so a show of force was needed.

Jesus would show that the power to bring freedom would not come by means of worldly power, but be found in him. The people hailing Jesus as king were challenging Roman rule and seeing him as the one who could save them from the Romans. This, though, was not the kind of power to free or the kind of kingship that Jesus inhabited. That was made very clear to all when later Jesus was paraded before the crowd wearing a crown of thorns and the cries of the people in response became, 'We have no king but the emperor.' Being executed under a notice declaring Jesus 'King of the Jews' brought a humiliating and a forceful realization of who had power and who did not have the power to save. No wonder the angels were bemused and sad to see the approaching sacrifice.

The king who rides a donkey, not a war horse, turns our notions about how to bring about peace upside down. Jesus knew the danger he was in and offered himself to us as a pattern for living in dangerous times, personally and politically. We choose who to follow and the choice to follow Jesus is an inner decision to choose life. Jesus didn't show us that he could wield power over life and death, but that in the face of death and destruction it is possible to choose life. In the occupied territory of our world, with pain and hatred, we can live differently, live liberated.

This journey has to be taken for oneself and on a donkey, in peace with oneself and others. Inner peace can bring about external peace, but not force it. There will be times when it feels successful, as it did for Jesus and his followers on Palm Sunday, and times when there is danger and humiliation. Both are to be encountered on the way of peace.

In Christ, death and destruction is never the end of the story, but in order to experience the life beyond them, the journey has to be travelled. It's rather like the children's storybook *We're Going on a Bear Hunt* by Michael Rosen and Helen Oxenbury (Walker Books, 1989). When the family, searching for a bear, face each obstacle – the grass, the river, the mud – the refrain is always the same: 'We can't go over it. We can't go under it. Oh no! We've got to go through it.' Jesus went through death and God raised him from the dead. He fulfilled the responsibilities of bringing about peace as a king ought to, but the enemy he conquered was death. Charles Wesley (1707–88) in the Easter hymn, 'Love's redeeming work is done', captures this in the words:

Lives again our glorious king;
Where, O Death, is now thy sting?
Dying once, he doth all save;
Where thy victory, O grave?

Jesus, as king, protects us from the destructiveness of death and in doing so conquers it. He saves and delivers us within the experiences of fear and danger. He does this by going through it himself, by experiencing the fear and pain and showing us that God the Father has the power to raise him and us from the dead. His courage and trust in God sustain him and are an encouragement to us.

Jesus shows that he brings about the liberation a king does by showing us that it comes from inner freedom. A king knows he is of royal line, worthy and valuable. Jesus' sense of his inner dignity and call, as both human and divine, frees him to choose to act in such a way as to enable life and peace, to be the fruits of what happens not only to him but because of him. Such conquering and freedom is in a kingdom not of this world, of course, as Jesus explained to Pilate when he asked if he was a king. It isn't recognizable by the earthly trappings of power. Such earthly wealth and success are blessings to be enjoyed and shared, but they do not bring deep joy to individuals or peace to a people.

Jesus is instantly recognizable by the image of kingship, the crown of thorns, put on him to humiliate him and his people. It will be on Ascension Day that we overturn this image of torture, when we sing:

The head that once was crowned with thorns
Is crowned with glory now,
A royal diadem adorns
The mighty victor's brow.
(Thomas Kelly, 1769–1854)

When this king conquers death it is a golden crown he wears, enthroned in heaven, reigning with justice and mercy and interceding for us.

- Is there something that you know needs to be faced and gone through? Can you make the choice to do this and journey with inner peace?
- Is there a mark of humiliation that you can turn to a sign of victory?

Tuesday: money talks

> Then Jesus entered the temple and drove out all who were selling and buying in the temple, and he overturned the tables of the money-changers and the seats of those who sold doves. He said to them, 'It is written, "My house shall be called a house of prayer"; but you are making it a den of robbers.' (Matthew 21.12–13)

> When Judas, his betrayer, saw that Jesus was condemned, he repented and brought back the thirty pieces of silver to the chief priests and the elders. He said, 'I have sinned by betraying innocent blood.' But they said, 'What is that to us? See to it yourself.' Throwing down the pieces of silver in the temple, he departed; and he went and hanged himself. (Matthew 27.3–5)

The numbers that we see on our bank statements every month are one aspect of the power we have in society and over people, perhaps people we support financially, buy presents for or employ. The numbers also indicate the power we lack to do things, give or feel secure. Money also exerts its power over the one who has it and it talks because some people can be bought or influenced by being given money. We say that money talks; it carries weight so that those with money can get things done with it and get their own way because of the status it confers and its power to influence.

We all have power in some way or other. Jesus used the power of his presence and popularity as a teacher to act symbolically in Holy Week. He had ridden a donkey into Jerusalem to make a statement about his power being humble and peaceable, but also the power of a king. When he turned over the tables of the money-changers in the Temple and drove out those who bought and sold sacrificial animals, he was making a statement and in doing so he was forceful and dramatic. These symbolic actions come in a long line of statements made by God's prophets. They were consistent in calling on God's people to realize that God desired justice rather than sacrifice, and right living had to go with worship.

It was Jesus' claim to be king and his attack on the Temple that was the basis of the charges against him. These were trumped-up charges alleged in an unfair trial, but we find Jesus withdraws into silence when accused. In the face of injustice Jesus was silent, like a lamb led to the slaughter. If we want to follow the pattern of Christ on the road to the cross, this silence can be difficult if it seems to imply that passivity is the example we are to follow. The pattern of Jesus, I think, is to use what power or agency he has in order to open up a way to God in whatever situation he finds himself. This is often in the form of a challenge given in such a way as to invite a deeper response, such as when Jesus enters into a dialogue with Pilate and explains that his kingdom is not of this world. But Jesus does not attempt to use his energy with those who treat him only as an object, by ridicule and brute force; rather he keeps silence. Earlier in Jesus' ministry a woman had been brought before him, silent and accused of adultery. She was being used as an object to catch Jesus out. Jesus defends her, points the finger at her accusers and speaks to her respectfully. When he is in the same position as she has been, he chooses only to speak where his words can somehow be effective.

Judas was one of those people for whom money talked. He seemed to find it easier to relate to people through financial transactions and to get his way indirectly, rather than in communicating personally with others. Judas ceased to relate to Jesus personally. As keeper of the money he was aware of its power not only to provide but also to influence. When the woman used costly perfume to anoint Jesus, he spoke up for the poor, but we are told it was the money that interested him, not the plight of the poor or the expressed gratitude of the woman. Judas sought to force Jesus' hand, to force the situation in the direction he wanted, and this was possible because of his weakness around money. The religious leaders used this weakness to entrap Judas when he went to them. He was already using the power he had of being known as one of Jesus' disciples. Using his relationship with Jesus against him, symbolized by the kiss to indicate who he was, was to betray him.

Judas was taking a risk in going to the chief priests and elders. The risk didn't pay off. He lost control of the situation by using his power to force a situation. It didn't go as he expected and then went so much further than he wanted. For Jesus was not going to respond to force with force. He did not use his power to escape, and sought to defend his disciples only with his words when he was arrested. When it came to Peter raising his sword to cut off the ear of Malchus, one of the high priest's slaves, Jesus would have none of it and healed the ear.

Judas uses money, but he didn't do it for the money. Judas wanted a strong leader but wasn't willing to follow one with such inner strength. He wanted a leader to show himself forcibly to others, so that they acknowledged the rightness of the cause and got in behind it. He saw himself as furthering Jesus' cause, knowing better, but in doing this he doesn't relate to Jesus personally but treats him as a means to an end. The plan went wrong, and the chief priests and elders didn't care about either Judas or Jesus, so with violence against himself, he took his own life.

As Judas was trying to force things, Jesus went in the other direction and offered himself up, but without losing his inner dignity or ability to act with care and integrity. People were never a means to an end, objects rather than subjects, as we see in Jesus' words to the thief dying on the cross next to him. Jesus responds to him not as a criminal but as a person.

It can be easier to throw our weight around rather than to deal graciously with people. It can be easier to give a forceful opinion, rather than seek to set the atmosphere and tone so that people can flourish. In seeking to make a difference in our relationships and our world we need to be conscious of the agency we have and how we use it. We can pretend we don't have power. We may or may not have money. It may have power over us even if we have little. Speech and being silent are very powerful. Manipulating events because we think we know better can be dangerous, as can absenting ourselves from responsibility, as Pilate did, by washing our hands of it.

- Are there times when things become more important than people in your life, for example money, or an ordered house or regime? How might you see people not as means but as ends in themselves, human beings for whom Christ spent his life in order to open up the way to God?
- What does your attitude to your finances teach you about how you will approach future decisions around money? What will be your Easter offering this year?

Wednesday: beautiful feet

And a woman in the city, who was a sinner, having learned that he was eating in the Pharisee's house, brought an alabaster jar of ointment. She stood behind him at his feet, weeping, and began to bathe his feet with her tears and to dry them with her hair. Then she continued kissing his feet and anointing them with the ointment.

(Luke 7.37–38)

He came to Simon Peter, who said to him, 'Lord, are you going to wash my feet?' Jesus answered, 'You do not know now what I am doing, but later you will understand.' Peter said to him, 'You will never wash my feet.' Jesus answered, 'Unless I wash you, you have no share with me.' Simon Peter said to him, 'Lord, not my feet only but also my hands and my head!' Jesus said to him, 'One who has bathed does not need to wash, except for the feet, but is entirely clean. And you are clean, though not all of you.' (John 13.6–10)

So they left the tomb quickly with fear and great joy, and ran to tell his disciples. Suddenly Jesus met them and said, 'Greetings!' And they came to him, took hold of his feet, and worshipped him. Then Jesus said to them, 'Do not be afraid; go and tell my brothers to go to Galilee; there they will see me.' (Matthew 28.8–10)

The events of Holy Week contain a great deal of violence and brutality, not only on the part of soldiers but also for the disciples themselves. Jesus is tortured and crucified and our primary image of him is as a victim being executed. We might think that the body of Christ, when given, is only broken. However, during Holy Week Jesus is fully present in his body and inhabits it in such a way as to give and receive with gentleness.

Isaiah the prophet declares:

How beautiful upon the mountains
are the feet of the messenger who announces peace,
who brings good news,
who announces salvation,
who says to Zion, 'Your God reigns.'

(Isaiah 52.7)

It is Jesus' relationship with feet that several times brings peace in a week of turmoil. Jesus has his feet anointed and he washes the feet of his disciples. On the cross we cannot but picture his feet pierced with nails and later the stiff pale feet of the corpse. At the resurrection, he is recognized by wounds in his feet, and the women fall down at his feet, clinging to them and worshipping him.

Our feet ground us and put us in touch with our humanity. Feet reveal a lot about a person and perhaps this is why we can feel very exposed and vulnerable when showing our feet or having them touched. When you compare the fatness of a baby's feet not yet able to walk with the corns and bunions that reveal a lifetime of ill-fitting shoes, you can see how time changes our feet. Feet carry us and support us through life and they ache and smell, reminding us of how far and through what we have come.

Jesus did not push away the woman who approached him weeping, who touched and proceeded to massage his bare feet with expensive perfume. There are different versions of the story of this happening to Jesus, but in each the woman shows devotion and care out of a gratitude for something that Jesus has done for her. Rather than be embarrassed by and rejecting of the excessive gesture, he is humble and protects her vulnerability because he is grounded and he knows who he is. Jesus can be touched, be secure and safe, even when a woman with a risky reputation anoints him. He can receive from her because he is aware of his own needs, for comfort and relaxation, and because he can see what it means to her to be able to thank him and be close to him. It isn't always easy to receive thanks or affection. Jesus is centred and present and because of his inner security he doesn't need to dominate or control. To receive is a gift he can offer, one that brings about further healing. He doesn't pull away from her, but respects her dignity when in tears. Equally significant in their relationship, however, is that she offers him an anointing which he understands is for his burial. Aware of the danger of death and what he will be subject to physically, he gains strength as he receives from her.

It is perhaps this woman's action that spurs Jesus to wash his disciples' feet at the beginning of the Passover meal. He wants to teach them about loving one another just as he loves them and of the importance of serving one another, of being able to give and to receive. It is common for us to think that we must be independent and self-sufficient and that to be so is a strength, but this is not the way of Jesus.

Peter wasn't going to allow Jesus, his superior, to wash his feet, like a servant. Jesus told him it was necessary to receive this from him and so Peter wanted a bath. Peter swung from feeling he wasn't worthy to have Jesus do it, to not being worthy unless he was completely washed, but Jesus does not let him take refuge in these extremes. Jesus was teaching about the importance of giving and receiving, about mutuality and the recognition that even if there is love, human beings do fail each other. Jesus, of course, would have washed Judas's feet. He showed Judas that he loved him, as well as later making it clear he knew he was set to betray him. Judas was not able to realize the depth of that love, and the tragedy in this was not that he betrayed Jesus but that he took his own life, feeling unable to come back. Peter and the others, however, having scattered, in their shame and vulnerability remembered the lesson of needing to receive love.

When tortured, stripped and executed, Jesus was physically vulnerable. Perhaps he was able to remember that he had been vulnerable having his feet anointed and in washing feet, but then he had not been an object, done to by others, but a person able to give and receive. Those experiences were expressions of intimacy and care that perhaps he was able to carry within him when he remembered them later, so that they could strengthen him.

It was having seen the angel at the tomb that the two Marys met Jesus on the path and held on to his wounded feet. Jesus told Mary Magdalene, who may have been the one who anointed him, not to cling (John 20.17). That can seem quite a shocking thing for him to say, but I think it enables her to move deeper into gaining her sense of dignity and purpose in her life, which had begun with Jesus. Jesus was able both to invite closeness and by the offering of his physical risen presence to enable confidence for these women to go and declare that he was risen.

Jesus gave his body for the life of the world. Fully present and vulnerable as a human being, he brought about wholeness and peace by feet that were beautiful, not because there were no wounds, but because God so loved the world.

- What might you receive from others, and for their sake, while being open to finding it a blessing?

Maundy Thursday: the past, the Last Supper and the future

> Then he took a loaf of bread, and when he had given thanks, he broke it and gave it to them, saying, 'This is my body, which is given for you. Do this in remembrance of me.' And he did the same with the cup after supper, saying, 'This cup that is poured out for you is the new covenant in my blood.' (Luke 22.19–20)

Perhaps it is the painting of the Last Supper by Leonardo da Vinci that we call to mind when we think of that night before Jesus died. The iconic long table appears in tapestry, on screens, and sometimes with other faces we recognize to make a political point or as a joke. My internal sense of the Last Supper used to be of a meal filled with a dreadful anticipation of betrayal, torture and death. But I have been profoundly surprised to discover that it is no longer the human failings and brutality that I dwell on, perhaps because these are to be expected and are always with us. What struck me one year, and has remained, is the dignity and tenderness of Christ in the way in which he prepares and provides for this meal and how he conveys faith in God, hope for the future and love of his disciples in such a way that the sustenance of that meal carries them through the dark places to come.

As a Passover meal, the occasion was already laden with meaning. It remembered God delivering the people from the last plague of the death of the firstborn by means of the blood of sacrificed lambs, from slavery in Egypt, across the Red Sea and on a long journey to the Promised Land. When we hear the account of the Last Supper, most often in church during a service of Holy Communion, we have those resonances, of course, as well as the echoes of the feeding of the five thousand and the heavenly banquet to come. We call the meal the Last Supper, but at every supper since that one, when Jesus is remembered, he is also present because he is risen. The past, the present and the future all interplay for us, in such a way as to make Holy Communion a sacrament, that is, an outward and visible sign of inward and spiritual grace.

Jesus created memories at the Last Supper by celebrating faith and hope and love in a time of danger, fear and uncertainty. He set about the preparations in such a way as to make the location secret and safe. He provided all that was needed for a splendid meal, which – as good food and wine does – nourished and reassured. Candles, conversation and foot-washing all contributed to the event. He was the manna, the true and living bread, which would sustain them throughout that long day: having just begun at sundown, it wouldn't finish until he was laid in the tomb. He was also the Passover lamb that would be sacrificed and halt the angel of death, his blood releasing humanity from the slavery of sin.

Jesus, as the host, provided for the meal and shared himself at the table. He knew the danger and was troubled, telling Judas during the evening to do quickly what he was going to. When Judas left, John's Gospel describes it as being night (John 13.30), but the darkness did not overwhelm the light that was Christ (John 1.5). Jesus knew he would need to pray alone to get hold of his fear and that it would be a struggle, so he asked for support. But in the midst of his own turmoil, he was able to convey wisdom and an incredible compassion to his companions. He was present to himself, God and to his disciples.

Jesus created memories that night by words and actions that would have power in the future. Not only the 'Do this in remembrance of me', which would last for ever, but words that enabled the disciples to get through the following days. He was one step ahead, perhaps more, but he gave the disciples pointers to the next step, sufficient to provide for them. We remember the prediction of Peter's denial, of course, but Jesus also told him to strengthen the brothers when he had returned, giving Peter the sense of a future beyond his failure (Luke 22.32). Jesus had already spoken of suffering and death on several occasions, but his analysis was not one declared baldly, without hope, but as part of a bigger picture of God's love for humanity and the mystery of sacrifice and suffering. He not only warned, in order to prepare them, but also revealed a future beyond things going wrong. In John's Gospel, we read a long account of what Jesus said at this supper, including what is known as 'the high-priestly prayer' where Jesus prays prayers of protection over his disciples and prays for their unity.

Maundy Thursday recalls the day when Jesus gave the new

commandment, to 'love one another as I have loved you', at the Last Supper. The day is a celebration of the gift of the Eucharist in the Church's calendar and traditionally priests go to the cathedral to renew their ordination vows to their bishop, before leading their people through these holy days. The gift of the Eucharist is the presence of Christ, given at that supper so as to convey faith in God, hope for the future and love. It is given, too, of course, to remember and make present the risen Christ at every supper after it.

In church, we are not generally nourished by a full meal, nor do we sit round a table when we celebrate the Last Supper. We know that many households find it hard to eat together frequently and so perhaps miss out on the opportunities to encourage, share and be nourished physically, mentally and spiritually by those older and younger. I have heard it said that the biggest mission tool we have today is a large table for people to sit round and be nourished body and soul.

- Where are the tables you sit round, at home, at work, in church? Can you call to mind, remember and make present Jesus at them, conveying his insight and care for a hope in and beyond difficulty?
- Are there tables you know where little is provided by way of food? Might you provide?
- Can you give something of yourself to a situation or act in such a way as to create memories to sustain other people?

Good Friday: standing at the cross

> When Jesus saw his mother and the disciple whom he loved standing beside her, he said to his mother, 'Woman, here is your son.' Then he said to the disciple, 'Here is your mother.' And from that hour the disciple took her into his own home.
>
> After this, when Jesus knew that all was now finished, he said (in order to fulfil the scripture), 'I am thirsty.' A jar full of sour wine was standing there. So they put a sponge full of the wine on a branch of hyssop and held it to his mouth. When Jesus had received the wine, he said, 'It is finished.' Then he bowed his head and gave up his spirit.
>
> (John 19.26–30)

To lose one's child not only breaks the heart of a parent but also goes against what is natural, for things are in the wrong order. The image of Mary standing at the cross has a long tradition in art, such as the sculptures of the Pietà ('pity' in Italian), the most famous being by Michelangelo in St Peter's, Rome. There is a long musical tradition of the Stabat Mater, the sorrowful mother standing, set by many composers such as Pergolesi and Palestrina. Icons and paintings of the crucifixion often have Mary, the mother of Jesus, and John, the beloved and traditionally the youngest disciple, waiting at the foot of the cross. I find it isn't easy to decide, should one need to, who, of the three, suffers most in that picture. Mary, Jesus and John all suffer and take a journey through death. The image of the three of them speaks profoundly into human pain as well as into its capacity, at its deepest, to be a way to God.

Mary, who carried Jesus within her, experienced the pain we feel when a family member dies, someone whom we have known for our entire lives and whose physical characteristics we may well share to some extent. A bit of us dies when that person dies. If we have been responsible for caring and protecting, then death shows us vividly that we have failed in that we could not prevent what has happened. Denial, guilt and anger are all common emotions at such a time. On the cross Mary cannot hold Jesus. His body has been taken from her and she cannot give the comfort that would be most natural to her.

Mary's experience of watching the suffering of someone she loves is a universal human experience. Here, arguably, is Jesus' first disciple, and certainly a resilient woman. We can look on Jesus with her and look on the suffering of those we love through her eyes. Mary knew before Jesus was born that he was a gift and not hers to cling to. There are times when we see those we love more as our possessions than children of God, free and called to flourish. Where we demand or give with hidden agendas – in our minds, words or actions – we diminish ourselves and them. We have to let go of what isn't ours, ever, or any longer, to direct. We must do what we are called to do, which is to love.

At Jesus' birth, Mary pondered all that had taken place. At a death, we too find ourselves looking back and in doing so can release the person and the past. As we open up our memories we notice the joy, see the difficulties and feel the pains. I often think of this way of mulling over our memories as picking up and opening out items of clothing to see what they are and holding them up in the light from a window. The light is the presence of God, which can be folded in with healing and love as I gently fold the garment up and lay it down.

John, the beloved disciple, sees a friend and hero put to death. When a peer dies we cannot but think of our own death and what kind of value we place on life. In sudden, violent and unnecessary death we cannot make sense of what has happened in our minds, perhaps ever, but certainly not in our shocked and confused hearts, at least for a time. We can be touched by any guilt or humiliation we sense is associated with the death. We can only make sense of what has happened as we incorporate someone's life and death into the way in which we live our lives going forward. That will reveal how we have been influenced by this life and this death, whether the person bore fruit in us or died in vain. John was to do this in the future, but on Good Friday he had no power to help.

On the cross Jesus is done to, a victim, nailed still and painfully so that he cannot escape, only die. Jesus doesn't let go until he is ready. When he does surrender, it is to God. In the face of the prospect of death, we engage in the struggle to live, not just to survive but also to say and do what we feel we need to. Often there are loose ends or things unsaid. Attending to these things helps to release not only the person dying but also those left behind. When someone has the chance to convey his or her compassion close to death, healing can come quickly for those who are present, with a sense of peace and rightness. Time has an odd quality when someone is dying, and things that might have been resolved decades ago can be settled in the hours left. Sometimes, though, death overtakes and time runs out. Jesus, struggling both to stay alive and to die, speaks to Mary and John, asking them to look after each other, to become mother and son, be to each other what he can no longer be to either.

Then Jesus has to look death in the face. Death does not have the last say, even on the cross. Jesus does not surrender in defeat but surrenders his spirit to God in trust. Death is ugly and bleak and Jesus feels deserted by God, crying out in the words of Psalm 22. He's at the end of what he can manage, but it is God to whom he entrusts his spirit and breathes out for the last time.

There is always a point at which we shift internally from pouring our energy into doing what we can, striving to make something happen, to knowing that we are in a mysterious new territory where we are urged and invited to hand over our life, or someone else's, to God. This may not always be in a situation that will lead to death, of course, but one where letting go of our claim and handing it over to God's grace is what brings about change and unexpected new life.

This journey that Jesus goes ahead of us on is a journey through death. Jesus trusts God and understands the inevitability of his call ending up in such a way. In this way we can talk about him being obedient to the Father. Jesus' deep acceptance of how things are for him, his deep openness to the divine, makes possible the dynamics of 'death working backwards', as C. S. Lewis has Aslan describe it, and the 'deeper magic' being called forth.

We know the end of the story today and we do at every death that touches our lives. The knowledge of the resurrection can transform every experience, but the same conditions will always apply. Whether our place is closest to that of Jesus, Mary or John in this Good Friday picture, it will be bearing the cost of love and trusting that God can enter into it that will have us go through death to life.

- Remember those who have died and entrust them to God's care.
- Pray for the world Christ died to save.

Holy Saturday: darkness

The grave that is given to you contains no further suffering;
it opens heaven and closes hell for me.
(Sung by the chorus in *The Passion According to St John*
by J. S. Bach, 1685–1750)

This is the night when Jesus Christ vanquished hell,
broke the chains of death
and rose triumphant from the grave.

Most blessed of all nights!
Evil and hatred are put to flight and sin is washed away,
lost innocence regained, and mourning turned to joy.

Night truly blessed, when hatred is cast out,
peace and justice find a home,
and heaven is joined to earth and all creation reconciled to you.
(Words from the Exsultet,
sung as the dawn breaks on Easter Day)

The menacing darkness over Golgotha when the sun was eclipsed at the crucifixion was of a quality quite different from the darkness within the tomb. The darkness in the tomb was a mysterious darkness and through the night of Saturday it gave way to a new dawn. The crucifixion took place on the rock of Calvary, which was said to look like a skull. The rock of the tomb, though secure, was contained and hidden rather than exposed. A tomb in a garden hewn out of rock was the place where Jesus' suffering was at an end and his body was laid to rest. Contained spaces provide refuge. In Scripture, there are many places like this. Noah's ark, Mary's womb and this tomb are spaces where God watched over, protected and delivered new life.

Delivery suites in maternity wings of hospitals are contained spaces for women to labour. They are, thankfully, rarely places of death, though the danger and fear of death is present, and night after night they are hidden places where through struggle and after pain there is joy and life. Fathers, like God the Father, I imagine, wonder how it is that love, desire and commitment to care have meant that the Beloved is put through such an ordeal. Mostly this experience of birth has been, until recent years, part of the private life of women – and of midwives, who are those 'with' the labouring women, for one can't do this alone. Time in the darkness of night has its own pace. The watching and waiting comes to an end with the cry that signals the first breath of a new life, and then, in my experience, very welcome tea and toast.

In the darkness of the tomb, the body of Jesus is raised by God to new life. God is faithful, and this hewn rock is a refuge against the enemy death. This raising is a strength and salvation, so much more than a physical event, just as the significance of a birth extends way beyond a delivery room. At a birth waters break and a baby is born. There is washing, holding, naming and bonding and then the baby goes through all this again when he or she is baptized into the new life of the risen Christ.

Perhaps we don't often think of the impact of the resurrection on Jesus himself. The tomb, dark and cool, would have provided safety in death, and in life a chance to rest a while and let the solidity of the rock support and soothe. But a tomb is a prison and it had a heavy stone across it. For Jesus it was angels, rather than midwives, who did the tugging and lifting when the time was right, and so he found that the stone had been rolled away.

In the deepest darkness of Holy Saturday everything changed. A cataclysmic shift took place from which for ever all creation could know that God brings life from death. A victory was won; a new kind of life began. In the darkness of the tomb, where time has a different pace, there was a movement of life itself. The Exsultet, sung in the darkness of the Easter Vigil, describes this night as blessed, a night where what is irreconcilable can be reconciled, where heaven and earth are joined.

Before the darkness lifts, the women are on their way to the tomb. Peter and John go too. Returning to a place full of the memories of death or pain inevitably fills one with caution. All these disciples of Jesus are surprised at what they find when greeted with the evidence that it's all come right. There is no death and destruction in the tomb; it is empty, and as they realize this, there are messengers from God to declare that Jesus and they have come through it all. They are told to leave the tomb and to live, telling each other what has happened.

Might there be experiences that, like the tomb, have held you imprisoned, in a place of death or stuckness? It may be that you are already aware of a shift happening for yourself. The darkness has its own pace. In suffering, going at the pace of a person suffering is important, for it aids the healing, physical and mental, which cannot be forced or rushed. The darkness, with hope that the dawn will come, may be the place for you to be at the moment.

It may be that you are aware of the need to engage and prepare for a new stage just about to come. The women got up and prepared what they needed to visit the tomb. Peter and John, too, having heard that things had changed had the courage to go and see.

Night gives way to day, and darkness to light. We experience the light when we respond to the signal that heralds life. At a birth the baby's cry tells us that the first breath has been taken, and everyone is relieved and overjoyed. It was Jesus' breathing on the disciples that brought them reassurance that he was alive, and the peace needed for them to realize that the darkness of death had given way to the glorious light of the resurrection.

- Can you identify an area of darkness that is giving way to light, or an obstacle that an angel might already have rolled away if you were to go and look?
- What signals new life emerging in your life?

Easter Day: the resurrection life of Easter

> Lift up your hearts, for Christ has conquered death!
> The night is past, the day of life is here!
> This is the night that gave us back what we had lost;
> beyond our deepest dreams
> you made even our sin a happy fault.
>
> (Words from the Exsultet)

The Exsultet is the Easter Proclamation, the hymn of praise sung just after the Easter or Paschal Candle is lit during the Easter Vigil, the service where in darkness Christians wait for the dawn and greet the resurrection. You can usually see the Easter candle at the front of churches all through the season of Easter, through the 40 days to Ascension Day and then to Pentecost, 50 days after Easter. Then, the candle is placed by the font and when people are baptized in the font, they are given their own baptism candle with the words, 'Shine as a light in the world.' Each baptism candle is lit from the Easter candle and symbolizes that the spark of new life ignited in our hearts comes through the redeeming power of the resurrection.

The Easter Candle, for me, is a reminder of what it means to be a mature follower of Jesus, a resilient Christian. Every candle, of course, can remind us that one small flame, even if flickering and vulnerable, sheds light in darkness. A whole church in darkness is illuminated by the flame of the Easter Candle, and as we light candles from it, the whole space is lit up. That's such an obvious and simple sign of hope, but my experience tells me that to be resilient involves these constant small reminders.

At baptism we are born again, but into resurrection life. An Easter Candle is dipped in the font, because not only does all human life come from God who as the creator said, 'Let there be light', but resurrection life brought about by Christ's redemption is ours as Christians. The children of Israel passed through the Red Sea and were freed from slavery and liberated to live in the Promised Land.

Our slavery to sin is expressed in the structures of our society and in the habits that trap us on narrow paths that lead to destruction. We enter into resurrection life at baptism, into the body of Christ, the Church, where we are called to help one another live this newness of life by our worship and by living compassionately together and for others.

Resurrection life is more than a belief that there is light in darkness. It is more than a resilient life of coming through adversity well, though it includes these. The Easter Candle is inlaid with a cross, the numbers of that year, and an Alpha and an Omega, which together declare that all time belongs to God. There is time, in Christ, for life, for forgiveness and healing, even when our own time runs out, or we are conscious that our progress is so slow. We can be resilient, but we cannot bring about forgiveness, peace and healing in ourselves or in our world. We need God's grace; we need to know that all time and all things belong to God. Every spark of life is initiated by God; all things come to completion in God. Jesus died for us, we say. Through the mystery of the cross and resurrection Jesus did something on our behalf, something we cannot complete ourselves, although in following in his way we participate in it.

Maturity involves recognizing that we are creatures and that God is creator. We are creative and made to love and live abundantly, but in our world there is darkness and light, death and life, and both touch us. You can tell which one is the Paschal Candle on Easter Sunday because it is the biggest one and it is new. Much of our celebration of Easter focuses on pulling out all the stops: loud organs and trumpets, huge lilies, churches full of flowers, so much chocolate. It can be hard to connect this with what happened in the few days before. The Paschal Candle connects Good Friday to Easter Day; it holds together the pain of the crucifixion with the hope of Easter. You can tell which one is the Paschal Candle all year, even when it's no longer new, or as tall, because the candle is pierced: it is wounded in five places. As the candle is lit, five incense grains are stuck into the wax to represent the five wounds of Christ, one in each hand and foot and one in his side. They are wounds made holy, because they have healed. They give life, from a place of compassion and empathy, a place which reveals that open wounds can become scars. Scars can be seen, and sometimes you are aware of them, but they are marks of experience, of coming through. The Easter

Candle represents the risen body of Jesus. The disciples knew they were encountering Jesus, risen, because they could see the wounds, and so see he was real.

We live as Christians, as Easter people. We always know the end of the story of Jesus, but it takes a lifetime and beyond to live it deeply. Adversity can help us grow as Christians and grow more mature. It is holding together the extremes such as light and dark, joy and sorrow, life and death, within our lives and with hope that is a sign of our growth in Christ. Resurrection life isn't a shiny, brand spanking new life, but a quality of living that can bear the darkness and within it find love and life.

A line of the Exsultet speaks of Adam's sin as a happy fault because it brought about the sheer goodness of Christ's redeeming work for us to participate in. There are many people who wouldn't change the suffering in their lives because of the fruit that came from it, but nonetheless we are rightly cautious about being glib about suffering, for it can damage irreparably as well as bring fruit. To speak of the happy fault, that both Adam's sin and Christ's suffering was worth it, speaks of the quality of the healing wrought by Christ and the life to be lived. God doesn't go in for naivety, but for dirty hands, wounded hearts, broken and loving lives that bear witness to the resurrection. This is a costly path where there will be wounds to bear, but in offering the pain and desolation to God as Alpha and Omega, there is resurrection.

We can see the risen Jesus today wherever there is the steady candle of hope and good works in human life. Our churches and charities shine out in this way. We can see the risen Jesus in every spark of new life, every new baby brought for baptism, every project, every gesture offered to reconcile and make peace. These sparks will ignite and burn steadily as we join our flames to them. And when we wonder where to look for the risen Jesus, we should search with our own baptism candles for where we can see woundedness. Drawn to the hurting places in our world, we will encounter Jesus in the hope we find is already there and the hope we find we bring with us, from God.

- Renew your baptism vows and shine like a light in the darkness.

Using this book with groups

Below are brief notes to guide a group leader in shaping a session based on each of the week's reflections and theme. It is highly desirable that people have read the reflections. I have assumed that a group would meet five or six times in Lent, depending on whether it meets in the first half-week of Lent as well as the first full week. Thus, I have split the material in **Follow** into two, but a group may well meet only once under that theme.

In each session, you can use prayers provided for that week. You may like to use different settings of Psalm 23 at the start of each session. I have indicated a picture or object you could bring to be a focus for prayer or reflection, an activity and some themes likely to emerge for discussion. You may wish to focus on the life of Peter in each session. If so, you will find that I have listed the reflections that refer to Peter in the next section of the book: Using this book in preaching and worship.

Follow 1: the desert

(You might combine this session with Follow 2.)

- **Focus:** stone, sand, ash. During a time of prayer, you might invite people to place a stone as a symbol of their Lenten commitment.
- **Activity (from the reflection: Make a straight path):** take a large piece of paper and write your name in the centre. In pencil write down all the things that fill your life. Include responsibilities, work, pleasures, people, domestic tasks. Go over in red the things that drain you and in green the things which nourish you. What is neutral go over in blue. Attend to the balance in your life and seek ways of making changes to enable you to live with a simplicity that means you can choose life.
- **Themes to discuss:**
  – beginning Lent;
  – desert experiences in our own lives;
  – what is resilience?

Follow 2: Peter

(You might combine this session with Follow 1.)

- **Focus:** something surrounding names such as a cup with a name on it, or a baptism certificate.
- **Activity:** your personal timeline. Think back as far as you can remember, and in the centre of the paper trace a line from then (or further back) to the present, indicating highs and lows – times of blessing and times of need. Think about where you have experienced God's closeness. Are you aware of patterns in your life that you might ask for God's grace to understand?
- **Themes to discuss:**
  – experiences of change and call;
  – names you might choose to grow into.

Flourish: building a house and a home

- **Focus:** the painting *The Light of the World* by Holman Hunt.
- **Activity:** draw a house where your peace could flourish. It will need boundaries; a doormat to wipe the dust of rejection off; a door without a handle – one that is for us to open, and to Jesus knocking; a tapestry or picture of a Bible verse for us to look at when slipping into rumination and self-blame.
- **Themes to discuss:**
  – hospitality: what do you value most when you are a guest in someone's space?
  – how do you make others feel at home in your space and at church?
  – Peter growing into discipleship by risk-taking and getting it wrong;
  – what challenges you to grow in developing strengths?
  – guard your inner life: the discipline and practice needed to shape our thoughts and responses.

Falling

- **Focus:** a broken object, the song 'Anthem' by Leonard Cohen.
- **Activity:** ask people to reflect on their own qualities and strengths, and those they seek to grow in by finishing these sentences:
  – I am a dove when I . . . [return home / seek peace];

– I am a serpent when I . . . [am alert / patient / ready to act and recognize when to let go of what I no longer need];
– I am a cockerel when I . . . [look for the light and declare the new day for others].

- **Themes to discuss:**
  – experiences of new life out of trauma, and difficult times of the day and in life;
  – Peter letting Jesus down and remembering what he had learned.

Faithful

- **Focus:** a picture of Epstein's Jacob wrestling with the angel, a kintsugi pot, a tangled ball of wool.
- **Activity:** prepare copies of an outline of a labyrinth for each person to follow with a pen.
- **Themes to discuss:**
  – people you know who have suffered and who bring about healing;
  – forgiveness, apologies and letting go;
  – when you know you are ready to be used again.

Fruitful

- **Focus:** grapes for each person.
- **Activity:** at prayer time, use grapes to ask what fruitfulness looks like in your life and to focus on:
  – someone to pray for healing for;
  – some healthy action to commit to / donation to a foodbank;
  – something beautiful to seek out;
  – somewhere we might be stuck and need 'fermenting'.
- **Themes to discuss:**
  – experiencing God through thin places, experiences, patterns and the presence of angels;
  – Peter and Paul, dealing with difference;
  – hospitality in churches;
  – the marks of maturity in the Christian life.

Using this book in preaching and worship

Using the reflections to focus on Peter during Lent and after Easter

These reflections on Peter could form a Sunday sermon series beginning in or just before Lent and into Holy Week:

- Called to depth (call)
- Named (rock)
- Take heart (walking on water)
- The reality of suffering ('Get behind me, Satan')
- Losing control (the three denials)
- The cockerel at daybreak
- Gone fishing

These reflections on Peter could form a Sunday sermon series in the season of Easter:

- Holding and healing (the three questions: 'Do you love me?')
- My story (suffering will come again; 'Follow me')
- Untangling and binding (forgiveness)
- Success without swords (Peter as leader in the early Church)
- Thin places (the vision of food three times)
- Peter and Paul (disagreement and difference)
- Angels (release from prison)

For Ash Wednesday, the Sunday before Lent and the first Sunday of Lent

The first four reflections are all suitable.

For Mothering Sunday

- The heart of God (using the three shapes as the focus)
- Gone fishing (this is on refreshment)

For a quiet day in Lent

The four reflections on the Prayer of St Columba work well together:

- Be a bright flame before me
- Be a guiding star above me
- Be a smooth path beneath me
- Be a kindly shepherd behind me

With a prayer group

These reflections recommend exercises appropriate to those seeking to deepen their spirituality:

- Voices in the silence (silence and the breath)
- Solid as a rock (imaginative exercise of God as tower)
- Losing control (the Welcoming Prayer)
- The buried treasure of our needs (NVC)